HTML and CSS for Beginners with HTML5

HTML and CSS for Beginners with HTML5

Mark Lassoff

LearnToProgram, Inc.
Vernon, Connecticut

LearnToProgram.tv, Incorporated
27 Hartford Turnpike Suite 206
Vernon, CT 06066
contact@learntoprogram.tv
(860) 840-7090

©2013 by LearnToProgram.tv, Incorporated

ISBN-13: 978-0-9888429-1-5
ISBN-10: 0988842912

Dedication

Thank you Kevin, who worked tirelessly to take the original video course and edit it into something that made sense. Thank you to Jimda and Alison, who made this book possible.

Table of Contents

About the Author

Mark Lassoff

Mark Lassoff's parents frequently claim that Mark was born to be a programmer. In the mid-eighties when the neighborhood kids were outside playing kickball and throwing snowballs, Mark was hard at work on his Commodore 64 writing games in the BASIC programming language. Computers and programming continued to be a strong interest in college where Mark majored in communication and computer science. Upon completing his college career, Mark worked in the software and web development departments at several large corporations.

In 2001, on a whim, while his contemporaries were conquering the dot com world, Mark accepted a position training programmers in a technical training center in Austin, Texas. It was there that he fell in love with teaching programming.

Teaching programming has been Mark's passion for the last 10 years. Today, Mark is a top technical trainer, traveling the country providing leading courses for software and web developers. Mark's training clients include the Department of Defense, Lockheed Martin, Discover Card Services, and Kaiser Permanente. In addition to traditional classroom training, Mark releases courses on the web, which have been taken by programming students all over the world.

He lives near Hartford, Connecticut where he is in the process of redecorating his condominium.

About the Course Producer

Kevin Hernandez

Kevin has worked at LearnToProgram since the company's formation in 2011. Kevin is responsible for the entire production process including video editing, distribution and testing of lab exercises. Kevin plays the French horn in multiple bands and orchestras throughout Connecticut.

Courses Available from LearnToProgram, Inc.

HTML and CSS for Beginners (with HTML5)
Javascript for Beginners
C# For Beginners
jQuery for Beginners
iOS Development Code Camp
Become a Certified Web Developer
PHP & MySQL for Beginners
iOS Development for Beginners
Objective C for Beginners
C Programming for Beginners
Android Development for Beginners
Creating an MP3 Player with Adobe Flash
AJAX Development
Python for Beginners
CSS Development (with CSS3)
HTML5 Mobile App Development with PhoneGap

Books from LearnToProgram, Inc.

HTML and CSS for Beginners
Create Your Own MP3 Player with HTML

Visit our web site at www.LearnToProgram.tv to enroll in our free and premium courses.

Chapter 1: Welcome to HTML

Chapter Objectives:
• Students will be able to identify various web development technologies.
• Students will be able to create basic HTML 4.01 and XHTML document structures.
• Students will be able to construct a basic HTML5 document structure.
• Students will be able to understand and implement basic HTML tags.
• Students will be able to use HTML head elements.
• Students will be able to understand the purpose of and create comments in HTML.

1.1 Web Development Technologies

Web development does not occur in a vacuum and there are several technologies and types of technologies that are part of the web development and web design process. These technologies are divided into front end (sometimes called client side) technologies and back end (sometimes called server side) technologies.

Front End Technologies: Client side technologies are those that are interpreted in the web browser. These include HTML, Javascript and CSS (Cascading Style Sheet Language).

Back End Technologies: Back end technologies are those that are interpreted by the server that stores the web page code and sends it to a user's web browser upon request. The back end technology usually creates HTML code and dispatches that code to the browser. Back end technologies include Java Enterprise Edition, PHP/MySQL, and Perl.

Each front end and back end language or technology fills a specific role or niche within the web application development process. These technologies often interact to produce the completed web page or application, but have a distinct role.

Technology/Language	Role
HTML	HTML is designed to format a document. *It is not used to produce the look, feel or style of a document.* HTML markup indicates the purpose of each element—not its page position or appearance. HTML is designed so that a document may be reused across media without a change to the HTML code itself. You may hear the term *semantic HTML* to indicate HTML that is produced with only the purpose of content in mind.
CSS	CSS is the design layer. Interpreted by the browser, it determines the visual appearance of elements. This includes both the appearance of the element itself and its position relative to other elements on the page.
Javascript	Javascript is the front end technology that deals with user interactivity. Javascript code can be used to validate user input, create drop-down effects, switch CSS styles dynamically and even make complex calculations.
PHP	PHP is a common, free, back end language. It is a powerful programming language that is the engine behind popular platforms like Joomla and Wordpress. It is most commonly used to process user forms, or interact with an external database. PHP is also the engine behind many eCommerce applications.
MySQL	MySQL is a common free relational database management system owned by Oracle. MySQL is used to hold data that is often used to produce dynamic web pages. For example, a MySQL database may hold the products within a catalog for an eCommerce web site

	and also production information and pricing.
Java Enterprise Edition (J2EE)	Java Enterprise Edition is a back end language that can be used to produce enterprise level web applications. J2EE is a powerful application development framework that is the engine behind some of the largest web applications in the world. J2EE works well when organizations are already using Java in other parts of their application development system.
Perl	Perl was the first server side language and was behind many of the original web applications and eCommerce web sites. Original development in Perl is not undertaken much anymore, but there is still a considerable amount of production code actively running in Perl.
.net Languages	The Microsoft solution for web applications is known as the .net stack. This includes the languages C# and Visual Basic. These languages require a PC for development and a version of Microsoft's Visual Studio product. .net Development is advantageous if you are running a homogenous IT environment.
AJAX	AJAX (Asynchronous Javascript and XML) is an application of Javascript that allows communication between the client and server to take place "behind the scenes." This results in a smoother, more desktop-like interface for web applications.

Question for Review

1. What coding technology implements the design of a web page?
a. HTML
b. CSS
c. Perl
d. XHTML

1.2 Hello World with HTML

In this section we'll create your first HTML page and display it in the browser. To create HTML code you must use a text editor.

NOTE: You must use a pure text editor—not a word processor. A word processor will embed formatting codes into your file that will be unrecognized by the browser when it attempts to render the HTML document.

There are number of free, quality text editors available for you to use. If you have a Windows PC you can use Notepad, which comes free with your operating system. If you are using a Mac or PC, you might elect to download the free editor Komodo which is available at http://www.activestate.com/komodo-edit. Other well-known, quality editors include Editpad Lite and Editpad++. It is not recommended that you use a WSIWYG (what-you-see-is-what-you-get) editor like Adobe's Dreamweaver for this course.

The code we'll examine in this chapter appears below:

Code Listing: Basic Document Structure

```
<html>
    <head>
        <title>Hello World from HTML</title>
    </head>
    <body>
        <p>Hello World from LearnToProgram.tv!</p>
    </body>
</html>
```

The file must be saved according the following requirements:

1. The file name should begin with a letter or number.
2. The file name should not contain any grammatical characters such as #, $ or <.
3. The file name may contain underscore characters.
4. The file name should end in .html or .htm. You may use either, but, please be consistent in your naming.
5. File names are case-sensitive, so be careful!

These requirements should be applied to all HTML files that will appear in the browser window.

Once loaded into the browser, the result should appear similar to this image:

In the HTML code, several tags and elements were used to create the document. First we will list the generic HTML terms and then discuss the intended function of each tag.

Opening Tag: The opening tag opens each element. It is comprised of the tag name surrounded by brackets. Examples: <p>, <title>, <body>

Closing Tag: The closing tag closes each element. It is comprised of the same tag name as the opening tag but is preceded by a slash. Examples: </p>, </title>, </body>

Content: Exists between the opening and closing tag. Content may be text content— which is output to the browser window, or other tags that are interpreted by the browser.

Element: An element consists of its opening tag, its closing tag and content.

Root Tag: The root tag contains all of the other tags and content that is part of the HTML document. In our sample document <html> is the root tag. All HTML documents use <html> as the root tag.

Keep in mind when authoring tags:

Whether tags should be uppercase, lowercase or mixed case has been discussed over the years. Different HTML standards have different recommendations and rules. What is most important is that you are consistent. **It is recommended that you author your tags using lowercase letters only, which is consistent with the current XHTML standard.**

Your tags should nest properly. This means tags should be closed in the opposite order that they are opened. While most browsers will forgive improper nesting and display your HTML code correctly, it is a best practice to nest properly.

Make sure all tags are closed. Again, this recommendation has changed over the years and the standards differ as to whether closing tags are required. However, the best practice is to always close your tags. There is no good reason not to, and this will make parsing the HTML easier for most browsers.

In the HTML code example for this chapter we introduced the following tags:

Tag	Purpose
<html>	Serves as the root element for the document. Identifies to the browser that the code contained is HTML code.
<head>	The head section of the document contains information about the document itself, and often, scripts. This information is not displayed in the document window itself, but instead is used by the page and search engines.
<title>	An important tag that has several purposes: The content of the title element is displayed in the browser title bar or tab to identify the document The content of the title element is used by search engines to index the page The content of the title element is used as the title of bookmarks, if the page is bookmarked by users
<body>	The body element contains all of the tags and content that will actually appear in the document window.
<p>	This is the paragraph tag. It is used to denote a paragraph within the page content.

Questions for Review

1. What tag does every HTML document start with?
a. <html>
b. <css>
c. <xhtml>
d. <class>

2. What section of HTML contains information about the website but doesn't display on the page?
a. head
b. body
c. xhtml
d. css

3. What tag contains content that will be used by search engines to index your page?
a. <search>
b. <find>
c. <head>
d. <title>

Lab Activity

Create an HTML page that outputs in the browser exactly like the following screenshot. **Notice that there are messages both in the browser window and on the tab at the top of the browser itself.**

Type this code into your text editor and then add the necessary missing code to produce the previous output.

```
<!DOCTYPE HTML PUBLIC "-//W3C//DTD HTML 4.01//EN"
    "http://www.w3.org/TR/html4/strict.dtd" >
<html lang="en">
    <head>

    </head>
    <body>

    </body>
</html>
```

Test in your browser by loading the file into the browser window. If the content does not appear correctly, correct your code and load it in the browser window again.

1.3 Basic Document Structure HTML 4.01/XHTML

In the previous section we created a basic document structure that can be applied to all HTML documents, but did so without adherence to any particular existing HTML standard. There are two standards that are recognized by the World Wide Web Consortium as of this writing. The World Wide Web Consortium establishes standards that are recognized across the web for HTML and other technologies.

For more information on the World Wide Web Consortium visit www.w3.org.

The two current standards are:

HTML 4.01: Introduced in 1999, HTML 4.01 was designed to replace previous HTML standards. HTML 4.01 was the first HTML standard to include CSS (Cascading Style Sheet Language) in its specification. This version of HTML recognized that HTML was not to be used to determine the appearance of the document, as this was specifically the domain of CSS. HTML 4.01 offers a slightly less strict interpretation of HTML than XHTML. In the HTML 4.01 specification not all tags are required to be closed, and upper and lower cased tags are permitted (as long as applied consistently).

XHTML: Introduced in 2001, XHTML was designed to more strictly enforce the rules of HTML. In XHTML all HTML code is also compliant with the general rules of XML (eXtensible Markup Language). XHTML, while still a current standard, was not greatly popular and work on a 2.0 version of XHTML has been abandoned. The major advantage of XHTML is that due to their internal consistency, they are more easily parsed by a variety of programs. XHTML 1.0 is both the first and final version of the XHTML standard—further work on a new 2.0 version of XHTML was abandoned in 2009.

For each standard, the basic document structure differs slightly. These differences mainly exist so that parsers and validators may correctly identify the type of the document.

The basic document structure for an HTML 4.01 document appears below.

Code Listing: Basic Document Structure HTML 4.01

```
<!DOCTYPE HTML PUBLIC "-//W3C//DTD HTML 4.01//EN"
    "http://www.w3.org/TR/html4/strict.dtd" >
<html lang="en">
    <head>
        <title>This is an HTML 4.01 Document</title>
    </head>
    <body>
        <h1>Welcome to HTML 4.01</h1>
    </body>
</html>
```

The basic document structure renders in the web browser like the image below:

Note the use of the <h1> tag. The <h1> is the heading tag. It is used to represent primary headings in an HTML document. Using the **default stylesheet**, headings are rendered from large to small. <h1> tags produce the largest headings while <h6> tags produce the smallest headings. However, it is best not to think of headings as size order—remember semantic HTML?

We don't use HTML to create a look or style, but rely on CSS for that. **<h1>** through **<h6>** tags are designed simply to denote the levels of importance of headings within a document. Very few documents use tags <h4> or greater.

The Default Stylesheet

Every browser has a default way that they present each tag. Later in the course we'll alter the way various tags look in the browser through CSS. However, without the CSS code the browser relies on the default stylesheet. To make things interesting—the default stylesheet that each browser uses varies in very slight ways. Often the variations are not immediately noticeable, but can prove to be a real annoyance over time. You

23

may want to note as you continue through the course where you see differences in the ways various browsers render content from the default style sheet.

In the basic document structure introduced above you will note the usage of the doctype declaration:

Code Listing: DOCTYPE Declaration

```
<!DOCTYPE HTML PUBLIC "-//W3C//DTD HTML 4.01//EN"
    "http://www.w3.org/TR/html4/strict.dtd" >
```

This line of code which appears towards or at the beginning of all valid HTML documents (with variation for different HTML versions) simply declares that the HTML document is written in HTML 4.01 strict and in English. The URL is the location of the document type definition—a document which defines the legal structure of HTML 4.01.

The basic document structure for an XHTML document looks like this:

Code Listing: XHTML Basic Document Structure

```
<?xml version="1.0" encoding="UTF-8"?>
<!DOCTYPE html PUBLIC "-//W3C//DTD XHTML 1.0 Strict//EN"
"http://www.w3.org/TR/xhtml1/DTD/xhtml1-strict.dtd">
<html xmlns="http://www.w3.org/1999/xhtml" xml:lang="en" lang="en">
    <head>
        <title>XHTML Basic Document Structure</title>
    </head>
    <body>
        <p>Welcome to XHTML</p>
    </body>
</html>
```

The XHTML document, when displayed in the browser, looks like this:

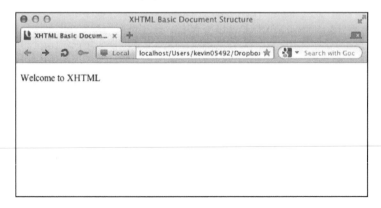

You will remember that XHTML documents must be legal XML. That requires the addition of an XML declaration at the beginning of the document:

```
<?xml version="1.0" encoding="UTF-8"?>
```

This XML declaration declares that we are using version 1.0 of XML and that the encoding is according to the "UTF-8" character set. This statement will be identical for all XHTML documents. The DOCTYPE declaration varies slightly from the HTML 4.01 version to properly indicate the version and DTD as XHTML.

In the HTML root node, you may notice another difference:

```
<html xmlns="http://www.w3.org/1999/xhtml" xml:lang="en" lang="en">
```

Within the opening tag you will notice several **attribute/value pairs**. These pairs indicate that we are using a specific namespace for our XML document. In this case, its the XML namespace. It's not critical you understand the idea of namespace in this context—its purpose is basically vestigial at this point. However, you will see the concept of attribute value pairs again.

Often within opening tags you will see a set of attribute value pairs. An equal sign always follows the attribute and the value will always be surrounded by quotes. The purpose of an attribute value pair is to modify the tag in some way. For now, just be familiar with the structure within the opening tag of an element.

Questions for Review

1. In order to establish what version of HTML you are using in your webpage, what declaration should you begin your webpage with?
a. <!HTMLTYPE
b. <!XHTMLTYPE
c. <!DOCTYPE
d. <VERSION

2. When using XHTML code, with which of these should you begin your document?
a. A language declaration.
b. A W3 declaration.
c. A HTML declaration.
d. A XML declaration.

Lab Activity

This coding activity explores the importance of using comments in your HTML code. Follow the directions to create an HTML document that has embedded comments.

Create an HTML document
Use separate <p> tags to display your name, address and phone number.
Use comment tags to create three separate lines of comments.
In one comment, identify who you are and the (potentially fictional) company you work for.
Identify the purpose of the page in another comment.
Finally, create a comment that identifies the function of a line of code.

This is what your output should look like:

file:///Users/BrettLassoff/Desktop/Labs/HTML/HTML%

My Name is

Brett Lassoff

I Live On

2 Charlie Rd. Vernon CT 06090

My Phone Number Is

5505555555

Ready

1.4 Basic Document Structure HTML5

Believe it or not, HTML5—which will become a provisional standard in 2014—offers a simplified version of the basic document structure. With the DOCTYPE declaration shortened and the XML declaration eliminated, you are down to a more bare-bones structure:

Code Listing: HTML5 Basic Document Structure

```
<!DOCTYPE html>
<html>
    <head>
        <title>HTML5 Basic Document Structure</title>
    </head>
    <body>
        <p>This is an html 5 document</p>
    </body>
</html>
```

Rendered in the browser, the HTML5 basic document structure appears like this:

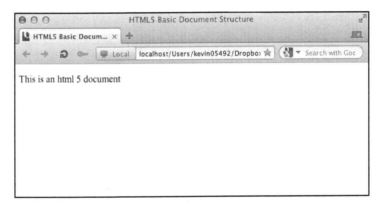

It's important to note that the browser does not alter its behavior or the way it interprets tags based on the basic document structure version that you use. These structures simply make the document valid and declare the HTML standard that you are using.

You can validate your code and ensure it complies with a particular existing standard by pasting your code into the text box located at: http://validator.w3.org/#validate_by_input

27

Questions for Review

Circle the correct answer for each multiple-choice question.

1. In HTML5, what declaration do you start the code with?
a. <!DOCTYPE html>
b. <htmltype html>
c. <!Version HTML5>
d. <!Content HTML5>

2. What language component of web development specifies the design elements of a web page?
a. HTML.
b. CSS.
c. Perl.
d. XHTML.

3. Which is the element to declare you are using the HTML 4.01 standard?
a. <!DOCTYPE HTML PUBLIC "-//W3C//DTD HTML 4.01//EN" "http://www.w3.org/TR/html4/strict.dtd" >
b. <!DOCTYPE html PUBLIC "-//W3C//DTD XHTML 1.0 Transitional//EN" "http://www.w3.org/TR/xhtml1/DTD/xhtml1-transitional.dtd">
c. <!DOCTYPE>
d. <!STANDARD>

4. What section of HTML contains information about the website but doesn't display on the page?
a. <head>
b. <body>
c. <xhtml>
d. <css>

5. What tag is used to create text that could be indexed by search engines and saved as titles to bookmarks?
a. <search>
b. <find>

c. <head>
d. <title>

6. In order to establish what version of HTML you are using in your webpage, what element should you begin your webpage with?
a. <htmltype>
b. <xhtmltype>
c. <!DOCTYPE>
d. <version>

7. What website do you need to go to in order to validate your HTML code?
a. www.wc3.org
b. www.w4.org
c. validator.w3.org
d. check.w3.org

8. If you are using the XHTML standard, what element should appear first in your code?
a. A language declaration
b. A W3 declaration
c. An HTML declaration
d. An XML declaration

9. In HTML5, what element should begin your code?
a. <!DOCTYPE html>
b. <htmltype html>
c. <version HTML5>
d. <content HTML5>

10. Where are comments visible?
a. In the browser bar.
b. On the title.
c. In the body of the page.
d. Only in the code.

11. Which symbol is used to begin HTML comment elements?
a. <?--
b. <!--
c. <#--
d. <+--

12. Where do metatags allow you to put information about your webpage?
a. Within the body of a document.
b. Within the title of a document.
c. Within the head of the document.
d. Within the comments of a document.

13. Which metatag often will appear as a description in search engine results?
a. <meta name="description">
b. <meta name= "keywords">
c. <meta name= "comments">
d. <meta name="author">

1.5 Using Comments in HTML

Since the introduction of computers, software and web development instructors have been telling students to comment their code and for just as long, software and web development students have been ignoring them. However, commenting your code is really an excellent habit and one that you should begin to implement now!

The browser actually ignores any comments that you place in the code as a designer or developer. So you might wonder, *Why bother?*

The purpose of comments is to document code so it is easier for you—or another developer who is looking at your code later—to determine what you were doing.

Comments in HTML start with the symbol: <!--

Comments in HTML terminate with the symbol: -->

In the example below, comments are used in two ways. First, the comments are used to place some documentation in the document head. Secondly, they are used to comment out the h1 tag so that it is ignored by the browser. This is a common technique used when debugging and attempting to diagnose problems in your code.

Code Listing: Using Comments in HTML

```
<!DOCTYPE HTML PUBLIC "-//W3C//DTD HTML 4.01//EN"
    "http://www.w3.org/TR/html4/strict.dtd" >
<html>
    <head>
        <title>How to Use HTML Comments</title>
        <!--
            HTML Comment Demonstration
            Mark Lassoff
            LearnToProgram.tv
            mark@learntoprogram.tv
        -->
    </head>
    <body>
        <!--
        <h1>Welcome to our page</h1>
        -->
        <p>You are almost done with the chapter one lectures!</p>
    </body>
</html>
```

As you can see, the comments cause the h1 tag to be ignored, but otherwise have no effect on the display of the document:

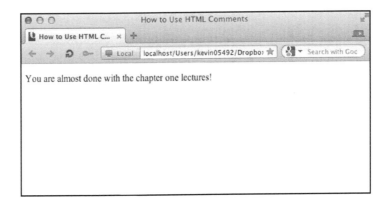

You are almost done with the chapter one lectures!

Questions for Review

1. Where are comments visible?
a. In the browser bar.
b. On the title.
c. In the body of the page.
d. Only in the code listing.

2. What symbol is used to begin HTML comments?
a. <?--
b. <!--
c. <#--
d. <+--

Lab Activity

In this lab activity, your goal is to create a fully functional HTML 4.01 document, containing many of the elements that were discussed in the chapter. Then convert that document into an HTML5 document.

Create an HTML 4.01 basic document structure that displays your name, address and phone number in separate paragraph, <p>, tags. Point your browser at http://validator.w3.org/#validate_by_input. Copy your code into the large test area and validate it against the 4.01 HTML standard. Note any errors. If necessary, correct your code and validate it again until it is free of errors.

Modify the document created in the first step of the lab so it conforms to the XHTML standard. Go back to the HTML validator page and again validate your code. (Don't forget to click the "More Options" tab and validate against the XHTML standard.) Again note any errors. Correct them and validate again ensuring your code is correct.

Add the head elements to your document mentioned in lecture 11. Ensure they are correct and properly structured.

Convert your document to an HTML5 document type and display it in at least two different browsers. Note the way these browsers render HTML content differently.

1.6 HTML Head Elements

Head elements are designed to communicate information about your web page, but are not directly displayed in the browser window. These elements, which are used with the **meta tag**, are sometimes used by search engines to correctly catalog your page. Each search engine has a different and highly proprietary method of cataloging and ranking pages, and meta tags alone are not enough. What will complement this meta tag limitation is supplementing it with the attribute called **name**. The content attribute contains a value that corresponds to each name.

Some common meta tag names:

Name	Purpose
Description	Provides an overall description of the page. This is often used by Google and other web browsers and displayed directly to the search engine user.
Keywords	Establishes keywords for your web page. While these are often common Google search terms, it is widely suspected that these keywords are ignored by Google and other search engines to avoid keyword stuffing and other "black hat" SEO strategies.
Author	Identifies the author of the web page

You will notice that the http-equiv attribute is also used to declare the character set used for the page. This type of meta tag is not frequently used in contemporary HTML authoring.

Code Listing: HTML Head Elements

```
<!DOCTYPE HTML PUBLIC "-//W3C//DTD HTML 4.01//EN"
    "http://www.w3.org/TR/html4/strict.dtd">
<html lang="en">
<head>
    <title>Meta Tags Example<title>
    <meta name="description" content="This web page from the HTML
course discusses the use of meta tags." />
    <meta name="keywords" content="HTML meta tags, HTML lessons,
HTML video tutorial" />
    <meta name="author" content="Mark Lassoff" />
    <meta http-equiv="content-type" content="text/html;charset=UTF-
8"/>
</head>
<body>

</body>
</html>
```

In this screenshot you can see how Google uses the description meta element to supply descriptions for the different pages indexed on a web site:

Questions for Review

1. Where do metatags allow you to put information about your webpage?
a. Within the body of a document.
b. Within the title of a document.
c. Within the head of the document.
d. Within the comments of a document.

2. Which metatag will often appear as a description in search engine results?
a. <meta name="description">
b. <meta name= "Keywords">
c. <meta name= "Comments">
d. <meta name="author"

Chapter 1 Lab Exercises

1) Create an HTML 4.01 basic document structure that displays your name, address and phone number in separate <p> (paragraph tags). Point your browser at http://validator.w3.org/#validate_by_input. Copy your code into the large test area and validate it against the 4.01 HTML standard. Note any errors. If necessary correct your code and validate it again until it is free of errors.

2) Modify the document created in the first step of the lab so it conforms to the XHTML standard. Go back to the HTML validator page and again validate your code. (Don't forget to click the "More Options" tab and validate against the XHTML standard.) Again note any errors. Correct them and validate again, making sure your code is completely correct.

3) Add the head elements to your document mentioned previously. Ensure they are correct and properly structured.

4) Convert your document to an HTML5 doc type and display it in at least two different browsers. Note any difference that you see between different browsers when they render content in your HTML document.

5) Add a comment. The comment should include your name, the date the page was created and your email address.

Chapter 1 Summary

In Chapter 1, we discussed the basics of HTML, including different web development technologies and how each technology is used. We also reviewed how to declare different types of HTML documents, such as HTML 4.01, XHTML and HTML5.

We examined basic tags in HTML and how each tag works. You discovered how to create your own HTML page containing text. We detailed various HTML elements including the title and head elements. We also discussed how to add comments to your HTML code. After reading this chapter, you should be able to build your own basic HTML page.

In the next chapter we will discuss text markup and how to use CSS with HTML to style your webpage.

Chapter 2: Text Markup

Chapter Objectives:
• Students will be able to understand and apply HTML text markup.
• Students will be able to implement semantic text markup.
• Students will be able to use HTML5 markup.
• Students will be able to understand Cascading Style Sheets.
• Students will be able to style elements of HTML using CSS attributes.
• Students will be able to create a CSS style sheet and link it to a webpage.

2.1 Text Markup

In this section, we are going to look at **text markup**. Text markup is how we use HTML markup elements to structure text. There are dozens of different tags that are used for text markup and we will review how those tags are used.

The most common tag used for text markup is the **paragraph tag**. It is written as **<p>** before the text you want to display. The paragraph tag is a block level tag, which means that the text is going to stretch across the screen unless you modify it using CSS. We'll discuss how to do that at a later time.
Another important tag in HTML is the **
** tag. This tag inserts a **line break** and is useful for laying out your content.

Another common set of tags used in text markup are **header tags**. Header tags are written **<h1>**, **<h2>** and so on depending on the level of the heading. The lowest level header is **<h6>**. The larger the number of the header, the smaller the heading will be, but you can alter the appearance of the header tags with CSS.

Heading tags are rumored to be critical for search engine optimization. Search engines, such as Google, will pay attention to specific keywords in your heading tags to analyze what the website is about and index the website. You want to make sure to include headings on every one of your pages and include keywords in your headings.
You can also alter the text within a tag to change the appearance of output. One way to do this is by using a **<strong>** tag, which is designed to emphasize certain text and makes text look **bold** in the default style sheet.

You may be wondering why you simply wouldn't use a bold tag <b> to make the text bold. The simple reason is that as HTML has become more advanced, best practices have evolved to avoid using markup to control the look of content. Bold simply describes the style of the text, which is the responsibility of CSS. Another tag that is used to change the look of the text is **<i>** to create italic text. For the reason described above, <i> should be avoided in favor of **<em>**, which stands for **emphasis**, the tag used for creating italics text.

The following HTML is a good example of how to use text markup in HTML.

Code Listing: HTML Text Markup

```
<?xml version="1.0" encoding="UTF-8"?>
<!DOCTYPE html PUBLIC "-//W3C//DTD XHTML 1.0 Strict//EN"
"http://www.w3.org/TR/xhtml1/DTD/xhtml1-strict.dtd">
<html xmlns="http://www.w3.org/1999/xhtml" xml:lang="en" lang="en">
<head>
    <title>Basic Text Markup</title>
</head>
<body>
    <h1>This was rendered by an H1 tag</h1>
    <h2>This is a second level header</h2>
    <h3>This is a third level header</h3>
    <h6>This is a sixth level header</h6>
    <p>This is some text.<br/>
    This is another line in the first paragraph element.</p>
```

```
    <p>This is some more text</p>
    <p>This lesson was hosted by <strong>Mark Lassoff</strong></p>
    <p>This course is called <em>HTML and CSS (with
HTML5)!</em></p>
</body>
</html>
```

This is how the code will look when viewed in the browser. Notice how each subsequent header gets smaller and how the <strong> tag makes the text bold and the <em> tag changes the text to italics.

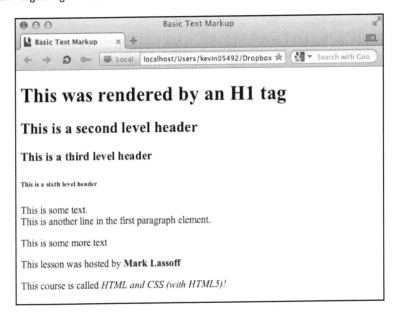

Questions for Review

1. What does the <br> tag do?
a. It creates a line break.
b. It creates new paragraphs.
c. It makes a line blink.
d. It puts paragraphs on two different websites.

2. What tag creates a second level header?
a. <h1>
b. <b1>
c. <h2>
d. <h3>

3. What tag would make text appear bold according to the default style sheet?
a. <em>
b. <bold>
c. <s>
d. <strong>

Lab Activity

Create an HTML page that outputs in the browser exactly like the following screenshot. Notice how each subsequent header gets smaller, and how the **<strong>** tag makes the text **bold** and the **<em>** tag changes the text to *italics*.

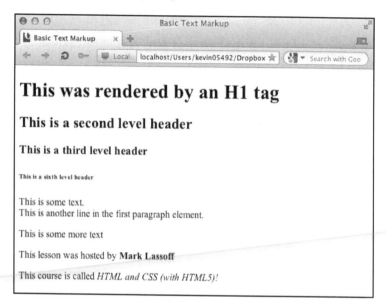

Type this code into your text editor and then add the necessary missing code to produce the output above.

```
<?xml version="1.0" encoding="UTF-8"?>
<!DOCTYPE html PUBLIC "-//W3C//DTD XHTML 1.0 Strict//EN"
"http://www.w3.org/TR/xhtml1/DTD/xhtml1-strict.dtd">
<html xmlns="http://www.w3.org/1999/xhtml" xml:lang="en" lang="en">
<head>

</head>
<body>


</body>
</html>
```

2.2 Div and Span Tags

In this section we are going to discuss two additional HTML tags. These tags are **<div>** and **<span>**. Div is an abbreviation for logical division, which is used to partition your content into different sections. When you see a header or footer on a website, it is usually contained in a logical division. Similar to <p> tags, <div> tags are block level tags. Div tags are most often used to isolate sections of content for CSS styling.

Span tags are inline tags. They don't create a new line but simply run continuously with the text block. The span tag doesn't affect the formatting, but allows you to section off certain text for formatting with CSS.

The following code is a good example of how to use the <div> and <span> tags.

Code Listing: Div and Span Tags

```
<?xml version="1.0" encoding="UTF-8"?>
<!DOCTYPE html PUBLIC "-//W3C//DTD XHTML 1.0 Strict//EN"
"http://www.w3.org/TR/xhtml1/DTD/xhtml1-strict.dtd">
<html xmlns="http://www.w3.org/1999/xhtml" xml:lang="en" lang="en">
<head>
    <title>Using Div and Span</title>
</head>
<body>
    <div>
        <h2>All about Mark Lassoff</h2>
        <p>Hi! My name is Mark.  I enjoy teaching different
computer languages.  I hope you are enjoying the course! I enjoy
teaching <span>HTML, CSS, Javascript, Java, C++, Objective C,
Android and iPhone</span></p>
    </div>
    <div>
        <p>Copyright 2011 | Mark Lassoff | LearnToProgram.tv<p>
    </div>
</body>
</html>
```

Notice in the following screenshot how the webpage is unchanged despite the <div> and <span> tags.

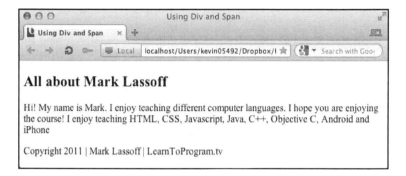

Questions for Review

1. What does the div tag stand for?
a. Logical division.
b. Paragraph division.
c. Header division.
d. Title division.

2. What does a span tag accomplish?
a. It gives you a break in the text.
b. It sections off a segment of text for the CSS to format.
c. It spans two paragraphs.
d. It puts two paragraphs on different headers.

Lab Activity

Create an HTML page that outputs in the browser exactly like the following screenshot:

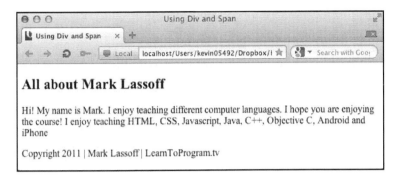

Type this code into your text editor and then add the necessary missing code to produce the output above.

```
<?xml version="1.0" encoding="UTF-8"?>
<!DOCTYPE html PUBLIC "-//W3C//DTD XHTML 1.0 Strict//EN"
"http://www.w3.org/TR/xhtml1/DTD/xhtml1-strict.dtd">
<html xmlns="http://www.w3.org/1999/xhtml" xml:lang="en" lang="en">
<head>

</head>
<body>
    <div>


    </div>
    <div>

    </div>
</body>
</html>
```

2.3 HTML5 Text Markup Tags

HTML5 introduces a generous number of new text markup tags. With HTML5, semantic markup is the primary concept. Theoretically, in HTML5, the markup should have no influence on how the text appears—we are simply sectioning off the document and creating an outline for that document with HTML.

One of the first and most useful markup tags introduced in HTML5 is the **\<header>** tag, which indicates that the section is the page's header. The header often contains various elements, such as the document's title or a welcome message or an image. The header tag sections off this area so that you can later style it using CSS.

HTML5 also features a **\<footer>** tag, which commonly contains copyright notices, legal notices and other information you would want to place at the very bottom of your page.

New HTML5 tags were developed by researching what id values developers were using for their div tags. For example, many developers were using \<div id='header'> and \<div id='footer'>, so in HTML5 the tags \<header and \<footer> were introduced.

Other new HTML5 tags include **\<aside>** which is designed to contain secondary content on the main page, **\<nav>** which is used to store navigational elements and **\<article>** which is meant to contain articles on the page. Once again, these elements won't alter the appearance of text, but are used to help style content using CSS.

This is an example of text markup with HTML5 tags.

Code Listing: HTML5 Tags

```
<!DOCTYPE html>

<html>
<head>
    <title>HTML5 Markup</title>
</head>

<body>
<header>
    <h1>Welcome to our HTML 5 Layout Site</h1>
    <h2>From the HTML and CSS (with HTML5)! Course</h2>
</header>
<aside>
    <h3>News from the Homefront</h3>
    <p>This news is going in an aside.  It is secondary to the
<mark>main content</mark> on the page.</p>
</aside>
<aside>
    <h3>More News from the Homefront</h3>
    <p>This is a second aside.</p>
</aside>
<nav>
     <p>Company News</p>
    <p>About Us</p>
    <p>Our Products</p>
    <p>Contact Us</p>
</nav>
<article>
    <h3>How to Cook for One</h3>
    <section>
    <p>Cooking for one is a challenge.  It can be both expensive
and time consuming if not done correctly</p>
    </section>
    <section>
        <h3>Recipes for One</h3>
    </section>
</article>
<footer>
    <p>Copyright 2011 | Mark Lassoff | LearnToProgram.tv</p>
</footer>
</body>
</html>
```

This is how the texts would look when displayed by the browser.

Observe in this screenshot how the tags did not alter the look or layout of the text but are more styled for future functionality.

Another markup tag used in the example is **<mark>.** It does not alter the layout of the text, but supports the display of the text as seen below. **Note that in some current browsers, the intended look by <mark> tag is already seen implemented such as in Google Chrome**.

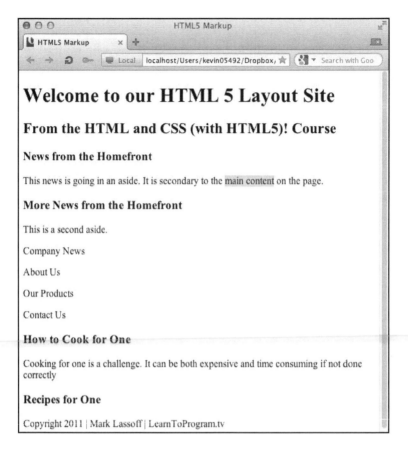

Welcome to our HTML 5 Layout Site

From the HTML and CSS (with HTML5)! Course

News from the Homefront

This news is going in an aside. It is secondary to the main content on the page.

More News from the Homefront

This is a second aside.

Company News

About Us

Our Products

Contact Us

How to Cook for One

Cooking for one is a challenge. It can be both expensive and time consuming if not done correctly

Recipes for One

Copyright 2011 | Mark Lassoff | LearnToProgram.tv

Questions for Review

1. What is semantic text markup?
a. The idea that tags should be called by proper names.
b. The idea that tags should be semantic.
c. The idea that tags should be named based on their function rather than their presentation.
d. A new type of tag that creates a header.

2. What markup tag would you generally use for the navigation of the site?
a. <aside>
b. <nav>
c. <header>
d. <footer>

Lab Activity

Create an HTML page that outputs in the browser exactly like the following screenshot:

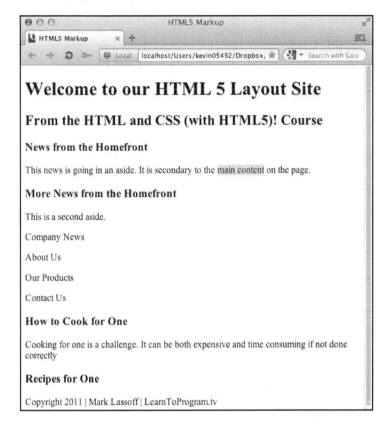

Type the following code into your text editor and then add the necessary missing code to produce the output on the previous page.

After which, view your code's output in Chrome and in another browser. Compare and note the difference.

```
<!DOCTYPE html>

<html>
<head>
    <title>HTML5 Markup</title>
</head>

<body>


</body>
</html>
```

2.4 Selecting Text Color, Font, and Font Size

In this section, we will discuss how to edit the color, size and font used for texts using Cascading Style Sheets. We first have to understand how CSS works.

There are three locations where you can place your CSS code. CSS can be placed in the style attribute of any tag. This is known as inline styling. For example, if you want to make an <h1 > tag content appear red, you would use **<h1 style="color: red">**. However, there are very few situations where it is a good idea to use the style attribute tag.

Colors on the Web

At this point, it is important to note that there are several ways to style the color of an element in HTML.

The most obvious and easiest way is to simply state the color name, as in the example below:

<h1 style="color: red">

But this method is very limiting, as most browsers will only be able to interpret the primary colors.

Another method is the RGB style. Almost all monitors and televisions display three colors (red, green and blue) in various intensities. This is how different shades are created on displays. Each level can be on a scale of 0-255, with 255 being the most intense. If you wanted a very intense blue in your first header, you would style your tag:

<h1 style= "color: rgb(0,0,255)">

By mixing the red, green and blue values, millions of color variations can be produced.

The last method is the HTML hex colors method. This method works in a similar way to the RGB method by starting with the # symbol and having the first two digits be red, the second two green and the third two blue.   What makes this system more complicated is that it uses hexadecimal numbers, which contain 16 digits.
The scale for hexadecimal numbers is: **0 1 2 3 4 5 6 7 8 9 A B C D E F**

A color is least intense at 0 and most intense at F. So if you wanted the most intense blue, it would be #0000FF. Your tag would be:

<h1 style= "color: #0000FF>

Hex numbers are very useful because they give us the greatest range of colors to work with.

Here is an example of using CSS inline. The code has been commented out so it doesn't currently affect the HTML.

Code Listing: Inline CSS

```
<?xml version="1.0" encoding="UTF-8"?>
<!DOCTYPE html PUBLIC "-//W3C//DTD XHTML 1.0 Strict//EN"
"http://www.w3.org/TR/xhtml1/DTD/xhtml1-strict.dtd">
<html xmlns="http://www.w3.org/1999/xhtml" xml:lang="en" lang="en">
<head>
    <title>CSS with Text</title>
    <link rel="stylesheet" type="text/css" href="intro.css" />
</head>
<body>
    <!--<h1 style="color: #b5cc8c">The Greatest Story Never
Written</h1>-->
    <h1>The Greatest Story Never Written</h1>
    <h2>A Story About Life, Love and Computer Programming</h2>
    <p>Lorem ipsum dolor sit amet, consectetur adipiscing elit.
Pellentesque suscipit felis quis dui <span
class="smaller">tristique</span> et dapibus orci tincidunt. Nullam
viverra nisl condimentum dui commodo feugiat. Etiam pretium mauris
accumsan arcu consectetur sodales. Pellentesque pretium, justo
lorem a urna faucibus et fringilla enim malesuada. Sed porttitor
accumsan tincidunt. Integer cursus convallis tortor vitae
adipiscing. Maecenas rhoncus scelerisque elit, vel adipiscing eros
tristique id. Curabitur suscipit commodo porttitor. Aliquam quis
nibh eros.</p>

    <p>Aliquam ac nunc enim, <span class="smaller">quis tempus
massa.</span> Morbi eu leo sed tortor pharetra ornare id varius
erat. Curabitur volutpat dignissim metus, ac porta ante vestibulum
ut. Cum sociis natoque penatibus et magnis dis parturient montes,
nascetur ridiculus mus. Sed ut erat ipsum. Ut facilisis facilisis
eros, ac condimentum orci varius sed. Nulla lorem quam, blandit
non, ullamcorper vitae velit. In eget urna tellus, at congue dui.
Vestibulum auctor tellus at lorem laoreet at ullamcorper enim
suscipit. Curabitur bibendum lacinia scelerisque. Donec euismod
purus ut mi consequat suscipit. Etiam in ante tortor, in ultrices
ante.</p>
    <p>In hac habitasse platea dictumst. Donec interdum commodo ornare.
Suspendisse eget eros est, eu blandit enim. Class aptent taciti
sociosqu ad litora torquent per conubia nostra, per inceptos
himenaeos. Nunc et nulla libero, at tempor mi. Curabitur non tellus
in sapien porta egestas at non mi. Praesent et lorem tortor. Nam
adipiscing est eu urna elementum rhoncus. Nullam volutpat hendrerit
dui, vel vestibulum odio sollicitudin eu. Suspendisse felis leo,
tristique in rutrum ultricies, ornare sed risus. Praesent in leo at
mi pharetra ornare. Proin eu elit leo.</p>

    <div id="footer">Copyright 2011 | LearnToProgram.tv | Mark
Lassoff</div>
</body>
</html>
```

Another place to put CSS is in the head element of a document. This is a much more common place for web developers to put CSS code.

In order to place CSS in the head you must first establish that you are using CSS. Do this by using the style tag and type attribute:

```
<style type="text/css">
```

Once you have written the style tag you can define the element you want to style. Simply indicate the element. When you write your element using CSS it is referred to as a selector. You don't need parentheses or brackets when indicating the selector. Once you have established the selector you wish to style, you need to place the style attributes within curly brackets. The following code shows you an example of how to do this:

Code Listing: CSS Style Sheet

```
h1      {
        color: rgb(155,70,150);
        font-family: Georgia, Times, serif;
        font-size: 2em;
        }

h2      {
        color: rgb(10,50,100);
        font-family: Georgia, Times, serif;
        font-size: 1.25em;
        }
p       {
        color: rgb(0,0,185);
        font-family: arial, verdana, sans-serif;
        font-size: .75em;
        }
#footer {
        font-family: arial, verdana, sans-serif;
        font-size: .5em;
        }
.smaller{
        font-size: .65em;
        }
```

Notice how the curly bracket is on the same line as the tag, while each style attribute is on a separate line. While this format is not required, it does make your CSS code easy to read and maintain. Each style and value must terminate with a semi-colon to function and each set of styles must end with a curly bracket. You can style elements with multiple attributes, but be aware that when you style an element you are altering every implementation of that element in the document's HTML code.

There are many attributes you can use to change the appearance of elements. In the example above, we changed the font with the font-family style and the typeface size with the font-size style. Browsers may interpret the attributes in various ways, or users may not have a specific font available, so it is always a good idea to put multiple fonts in your styles.

There are also several systems used to measure the font size in the font-size attribute. Some developers measure the font size in points, abbreviated as **pt**, similar to the way a word processor measures font size. Other coders will also use pixels to measure font size which is abbreviated as **px**. This is actually a measurement of the pixel size of the font.

Another way to measure the size of a font is with the **em** attribute which is defined as a percentage of the user's default style sheet font size. If you wanted to create a font that was half the size of the user's default font size, you would use the value .5em. This means your font would be 50% of the default font setting. This method helps make your document more accessible to users with vision problems who may set a higher than average default font size in their browser.

You can also change the document style by accessing div elements. In our previous example, the div with the 'footer' id is altered. In the actual code the div is given an id attribute which is called by using the pound sign with the id value as a selector.

This is an example of how the div id footer is styled.

Code Listing: Styling Divs

```
#footer {
        font-family: arial, verdana, sans-serif;
        font-size: .5em;
        }
```

Spans are used to set aside a section of inline text for styling. In the previous example we have added a span element to our text. That span can be called in the CSS by its class for styling.

In the first sample code, note that in order to start styling the text within the span, we created a CSS selector with a period and the class name and created a class called **'smaller'** that was applied to a span element.

Classes and ids are similar—but with one important distinction. An id is designed to be used only once in a document, whereas a class can be applied to several elements. Ids, commonly used with divs, are generally designed for non-repeatable elements like page sections. Classes, on the other hand, are designed for a style you may use more than once, like turning something red.

This is how the above styling will look in the browser:

The third way to apply CSS is to create the CSS in a separate document. This method is great for keeping the styles consistent on multiple pages.

To use the external CSS method, you need to create a new document and add **.css** as the extension. For example, you could create a document titled **style.css**.

For an external style sheet you only need to write the selectors and associated styles. You do not need to include a style tag in the external document.

To include external CSS styles in any HTML page you use a simple link to the CSS file. This is an example of a proper link tag:

```
<link rel="stylesheet" type="text/css" href="style.css"/>
```

The attributes **rel, type** and **href** are all required, however, only the value of the href attribute will ever change.

The attached style sheet is the most useful and efficient way of implementing CSS as it helps maintain consistency throughout your web pages and doesn't require separate stylesheets on each page.

Questions for Review

1. Which RGB value would you set to, if you wanted purely blue text?
a. RGB(0, 0, 255)
b. RGB (50, 100, 250)
c. RGB (0,255,0)
d. (255,0,0)

2. Where is the cascading style sheet most commonly placed?
a. In the style attribute of the tag.
b. In the document head.
c. In the XML code.
d. In the Javascript.

3. What attribute within the CSS would you use to change the font within a tag?
a. font-size:
b. font-pick:
c. font-family:
d. font-choose

Lab Activity

In this activity, the CSS code has been removed from the HTML document. Add the necessary CSS code in order to make the document appear like the screenshot.

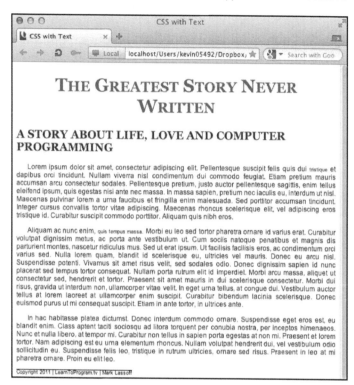

Note: We have used filler text (which appears in Latin) instead of real content. Since we're only attempting to learn styling, the content is irrelevant. Instead of typing this text you may download automatically generated filler text from http://www.lipsum.com.

```
<?xml version="1.0" encoding="UTF-8"?>
<!DOCTYPE html PUBLIC "-//W3C//DTD XHTML 1.0 Strict//EN"
"http://www.w3.org/TR/xhtml1/DTD/xhtml1-strict.dtd">
<html xmlns="http://www.w3.org/1999/xhtml" xml:lang="en" lang="en">
<head>
    <title>CSS with Text</title>
<style type="text/css">

</style>
    </head>
<body>

    <h1>The Greatest Story Never Written</h1>
    <h2>A Story About Life, Love and Computer Programming</h2>
    <p>Lorem ipsum dolor sit amet, consectetur adipiscing elit.
Pellentesque suscipit felis quis dui <span
class="smaller">tristique</span> et dapibus orci tincidunt. Nullam
```

viverra nisl condimentum dui commodo feugiat. Etiam pretium mauris accumsan arcu consectetur sodales. Pellentesque pretium, justo auctor pellentesque sagittis, enim tellus eleifend ipsum, quis egestas nisi ante nec massa. In massa sapien, pretium nec iaculis eu, interdum ut nisl. Maecenas pulvinar lorem a urna faucibus et fringilla enim malesuada. Sed porttitor accumsan tincidunt. Integer cursus convallis tortor vitae adipiscing. Maecenas rhoncus scelerisque elit, vel adipiscing eros tristique id. Curabitur suscipit commodo porttitor. Aliquam quis nibh eros.</p>

<p>Aliquam ac nunc enim, <span class="smaller">quis tempus massa.</span> Morbi eu leo sed tortor pharetra ornare id varius erat. Curabitur volutpat dignissim metus, ac porta ante vestibulum ut. Cum sociis natoque penatibus et magnis dis parturient montes, nascetur ridiculus mus. Sed ut erat ipsum. Ut facilisis facilisis eros, ac condimentum orci varius sed. Nulla lorem quam, blandit id scelerisque eu, ultricies vel mauris. Donec eu arcu nisl. Suspendisse potenti. Vivamus sit amet risus velit, sed sodales odio. Donec dignissim sapien id nunc placerat sed tempus tortor consequat. Nullam porta rutrum elit id imperdiet. Morbi arcu massa, aliquet ut consectetur sed, hendrerit et tortor. Praesent sit amet mauris in dui scelerisque consectetur. Morbi dui risus, gravida ut interdum non, ullamcorper vitae velit. In eget urna tellus, at congue dui. Vestibulum auctor tellus at lorem laoreet at ullamcorper enim suscipit. Curabitur bibendum lacinia scelerisque. Donec euismod purus ut mi consequat suscipit. Etiam in ante tortor, in ultrices ante.</p>

<p>In hac habitasse platea dictumst. Donec interdum commodo ornare. Suspendisse eget eros est, eu blandit enim. Class aptent taciti sociosqu ad litora torquent per conubia nostra, per inceptos himenaeos. Nunc et nulla libero, at tempor mi. Curabitur non tellus in sapien porta egestas at non mi. Praesent et lorem tortor. Nam adipiscing est eu urna elementum rhoncus. Nullam volutpat hendrerit dui, vel vestibulum odio sollicitudin eu. Suspendisse felis leo, tristique in rutrum ultricies, ornare sed risus. Praesent in leo at mi pharetra ornare. Proin eu elit leo.</p>

<div id="footer">Copyright 2011 | LearnToProgram.tv | Mark Lassoff</div>
</body>
</html>

2.5 Text Alignment, Decoration, Indentation and Text Transformation

In this section we are going to discuss a few more ways you can adjust your text appearance using CSS. Below, we have our document from the previous subchapter, which is linked to a CSS document named 'intro.css'.

Code Listing: CSS Example

```
<?xml version="1.0" encoding="UTF-8"?>
<!DOCTYPE html PUBLIC "-//W3C//DTD XHTML 1.0 Strict//EN"
"http://www.w3.org/TR/xhtml1/DTD/xhtml1-strict.dtd">
<html xmlns="http://www.w3.org/1999/xhtml" xml:lang="en" lang="en">
<head>
    <title>CSS with Text</title>
    <link rel="stylesheet" type="text/css" href="intro.css" />
</head>
<body>
    <!--<h1 style="color: #b5cc8c">The Greatest Story Never
Written</h1>-->
    <h1>The Greatest Story Never Written</h1>
    <h2>A Story About Life, Love and Computer Programming</h2>
    <p>Lorem ipsum dolor sit amet, consectetur adipiscing elit.
Pellentesque suscipit felis quis dui <span
class="smaller">tristique</span> et dapibus orci tincidunt. Nullam
viverra nisl condimentum dui commodo feugiat. Etiam pretium mauris
accumsan arcu consectetur sodales. Pellentesque pretium, justo
auctor pellentesque sagittis, enim tellus eleifend ipsum, quis
egestas nisi ante nec massa. In massa sapien, pretium nec iaculis
eu, interdum ut nisl. Maecenas pulvinar lorem a urna faucibus et
fringilla enim malesuada. Sed porttitor accumsan tincidunt. Integer
cursus convallis tortor vitae adipiscing. Maecenas rhoncus
scelerisque elit, vel adipiscing eros tristique id. Curabitur
suscipit commodo porttitor. Aliquam quis nibh eros.</p>

    <p>Aliquam ac nunc enim, <span class="smaller">quis tempus
massa.</span> Morbi eu leo sed tortor pharetra ornare id varius
erat. Curabitur volutpat dignissim metus, ac porta ante vestibulum
ut. Cum sociis natoque penatibus et magnis dis parturient montes,
nascetur ridiculus mus. Sed ut erat ipsum. Ut facilisis facilisis
eros, ac condimentum orci varius sed. Nulla lorem quam, blandit id
scelerisque eu, ultricies vel mauris. Donec eu arcu nisl.
Suspendisse potenti. Vivamus sit amet risus velit, sed sodales
odio. Donec dignissim sapien id nunc placerat sed tempus tortor
consequat. Nullam porta rutrum elit id imperdiet. Morbi arcu massa,
aliquet ut consectetur sed, hendrerit et tortor. Praesent sit amet
mauris in dui scelerisque consectetur. Morbi dui risus, gravida ut
interdum non, ullamcorper vitae velit. In eget urna tellus, at
congue dui. Vestibulum auctor tellus at lorem laoreet at
ullamcorper enim suscipit. Curabitur bibendum lacinia scelerisque.
Donec euismod purus ut mi consequat suscipit. Etiam in ante tortor,
in ultrices ante.</p>
```

```
<p>In hac habitasse platea dictumst. Donec interdum commodo ornare.
Suspendisse eget eros est, eu blandit enim. Class aptent taciti
sociosqu ad litora torquent per conubia nostra, per inceptos
himenaeos. Nunc et nulla libero, at tempor mi. Curabitur non tellus
in sapien porta egestas at non mi. Praesent et lorem tortor. Nam
adipiscing est eu urna elementum rhoncus. Nullam volutpat hendrerit
dui, vel vestibulum odio sollicitudin eu. Suspendisse felis leo,
tristique in rutrum ultricies, ornare sed risus. Praesent in leo at
mi pharetra ornare. Proin eu elit leo.</p>

<div id="footer">Copyright 2011 | LearnToProgram.tv | Mark
Lassoff</div>
</body>
</html>
```

You can align text with the '**text-align**' attribute. If you want to center the text, use the "**text-align: center**" attribute. You can also align text using the "**text-align: justify**" attribute. Using 'justify' as your text-align value aligns the text on both the left side and right side of the document.

The '**text-decoration**' style offers multiple options for text appearance, including "**text-decoration: underline**" and "**text-decoration: strikethrough**".

If you want your paragraphs to appear indented, use the "**text-indent**" attribute and indicate how many pixels you want the element to be indented.

Another attribute is "**text-transform**". You can use this attribute to adjust the case of the text. You can select all uppercase text, all lowercase text or sentence case text.

One interesting attribute is "**font-variant**" which allows you to transform the font in various ways. In this example, we have used "font-variant" to turn all lowercase letters into smaller uppercase letters.

Following is the CSS code for styling the previous HTML code.

Code Listing: Style Example

```
h1      {
        color: rgb(155,70,150);
        font-family: Georgia, Times, serif;
        font-size: 2em;
        text-align: center;
        font-variant: small-caps;
        }

h2      {
        color: rgb(10,50,100);
        font-family: Georgia, Times, serif;
        font-size: 1.25em;
        text-transform: uppercase;
        }

p       {
        color: rgb(0,0,185);
```

```
        font-family: arial, verdana, sans-serif;
        font-size: .75em;
       text-align: justify;
       text-indent: 20px;
       }

#footer {
        font-family: arial, verdana, sans-serif;
        font-size: .5em;
        text-decoration: overline;
        }

.smaller{
        font-size: .65em;
        }
```

This is how the above CSS code styling will look in a browser. **Notice the overline on the footer and the centered header.**

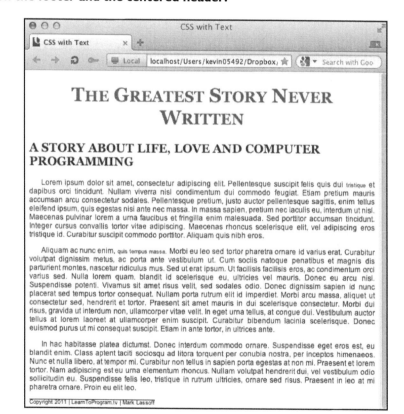

Questions for Review

1. What attribute would you use if you wanted to underline your text?
a. text-align: underline
b. text-align: justify

c. text-decoration: blink
d. text-decoration: underline

2. What attribute would you use if you wanted to decorate your text with an overline?
a. text-align: underline
b. text-align: justify
c. text-decoration: blink
d. text-decoration: overline

3. What attribute would you use if you wanted to indent your text by 50 pixels?
a. text-indent: 40px
b. text- indent: 50px
c. text- indent: 50pt
d. text- indent: 50em

4. Identify the function, purpose and, if appropriate, the output produced by each code fragment. Write your answers in the space provided.

4.1. color: rgb(10,50,100);

4.2. font-family: arial, verdana, sans-serif;

4.3. text-decoration: overline;

4.4. font-size: .65em;

4.5. text-transform: uppercase;

Chapter 2 Lab Exercises

Create a basic HTML document. Use markup tags and div elements. Style the document using the techniques introduced in the text.

Create a correct and standard-compliant XHTML basic document structure. Inside the <title> element place the text **Lab 2: Text**.

Within the body element create two <div> elements (opening and closing tags). In the first element, put an appropriate header element that contains the text content **"Places I'd like to visit."** In the second <div> element, place an appropriate header element that contains the text content **"Foods I like to Eat."**

Under each of the header elements, create a list of places you'd like to visit and places you like to eat using <p> tags, <br/> tags and other markup tags as appropriate.

Create a <style> element. Make sure to use the appropriate attribute/value pair with your <style> tag to ensure that browsers recognize your stylesheet correctly.

Style your heading tags as follows:

Font: Georgia
Font Size: 16pt
Color: Red 215 | Green 0 | Blue 0

Style the text in the lists below the heading tags as follows:

Font: Arial
Font Size: 80% of the default style sheet (Use ems)
Color: #0000AB

Using the correct CSS rule, center-align your heading tags and make them all capital letters (don't change the text content of the elements.)

Chapter 2 Summary

In this chapter, we discussed how to use **HTML text markup**. You learned various methods for altering text using HTML. We also reviewed the new tags that will be available in HTML5. You discovered how to use **<div>** and **<span>** tags as well.

This chapter also gave an introduction and **overview of using CSS to style** your HTML. We discussed the three methods for implementing CSS in your HTML and which method was appropriate depending on the situation. We also reviewed several attributes for **styling text**, including attributes for **changing the color and font**. In future chapters, we will go into greater detail on how to use CSS to make your websites look neat and professional.

In the following chapter, we will discuss how to organize your text using lists. You will learn how to create ordered and unordered lists and style your lists using CSS.

List of Tags, Styles and terminologies introduced

Tag, Style or Terminology	Definition
Text markup	A general term describing the HTML elements integrated into content.
<h1>	A first level HTML heading.
<h2>	A second level HTML heading.
<h3>	A third level HTML heading.
<em>	A tag that denotes emphasized text.
<strong>	A tag that denotes strong text.
<span>	A tag that is used to denote a portion of inline text for formatting with CSS.
<div>	A tag that divides a block-level section of text.
Inline tag	A category of tags that don't create a new line but simply run continuously with the text block.
<header>	An HTML5 tag meant to section off text as the header of the document.
<footer>	An HTML5 tag meant to section off text as the footer of the document.
<aside>	An HTML5 tag meant to place some text aside from the main article. Usually this is used for content that is ancillary.
<nav>	An HTML5 tag meant to section text and/or images as the navigation element of the document. Frequently the menu bar would be stored within a <nav> element.
<article>	An HTML5 tag meant to section off text as an article within the document. It may be used multiple times within an HTML document. It can also be used to denote elements like blog entries or user posts.
inline styling	When CSS is placed directly in the tag using the style attribute.
RGB	A color system used in CSS that uses three color levels (red, green and blue) to create a color. Each RGB level can be from 0-255 with 255 being the most intense and 0 being the least intense.
Hex Colors	A color system used in CSS that works in a similar way to the RGB method by starting with the # symbol and having the first two digits be red, the second two green and the third two blue. This method uses hexadecimal numbers on a scale 0 though FF. 0 is the least intense and FF is the most. FF represents a decimal value of 255.

Chapter 3: Working with Lists

Chapter Objectives:
•Students will be able to create ordered and unordered lists.
•Students will be able to alter the bullets of the lists.
•Students will be able to style the lists using CSS.

3.1 Ordered Lists

In this section we are going to discuss the concept of ordered lists. Ordered lists are used when there are a finite number of items that you want to list.

Creating an ordered list is pretty simple. You start the ordered list with the **<ol>** tag. Each list item starts and ends with the **<li>** tag.

The browser numbers each item in an ordered list. However, you can also style the ordered list using HTML style tags. The attribute '**type**' allow you to use different numbering systems or style for your lists. See table below:

Attribute Type for <ol> tag	Precedes each list type with:
<ol> (default)	Numbers
<ol type="I">	Uppercase Roman numeral
<ol type="i">	Lowercase Roman numeral
<ol type="A">	Uppercase letters/English alphabet
<ol type="a">	Lowercase letters/English alphabet

The following examples demonstrate how each of the tags and attributes are used, followed by an image capture of how it will look after using each attribute.

Code Listing: Ordered Lists - default

```
<?xml version="1.0" encoding="UTF-8"?>
<!DOCTYPE html PUBLIC "-//W3C//DTD XHTML 1.0 Strict//EN"
"http://www.w3.org/TR/xhtml1/DTD/xhtml1-strict.dtd">
<html xmlns="http://www.w3.org/1999/xhtml" xml:lang="en"
lang="en">
<head>
    <title>Ordered Lists</title>
</head>
<body>
    <h2>My Five Favorite Cities</h2>
    <ol>
        <li>New York City</li>
        <li>London</li>
        <li>San Francisco</li>
        <li>Salt Lake City</li>
        <li>Honolulu, Hawaii</li>
    </ol>
</body>
</html>
```

This is how a default ordered list **<ol>** looks when viewed in the browser:

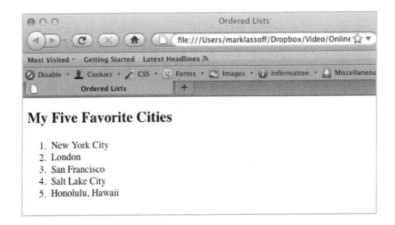

Code Listing: Ordered Lists – type='I'

```
<?xml version="1.0" encoding="UTF-8"?>
<!DOCTYPE html PUBLIC "-//W3C//DTD XHTML 1.0 Strict//EN"
"http://www.w3.org/TR/xhtml1/DTD/xhtml1-strict.dtd">
<html xmlns="http://www.w3.org/1999/xhtml" xml:lang="en" lang="en">
<head>
    <title>Ordered Lists</title>
</head>
<body>
    <h2>My Five Favorite Cities</h2>
    <ol type='I'>
        <li>New York City</li>
        <li>London</li>
        <li>San Francisco</li>
        <li>Salt Lake City</li>
        <li>Honolulu, Hawaii</li>
    </ol>
</body>
</html>
```

This is how **<ol type='I'>** will look when viewed in the browser:

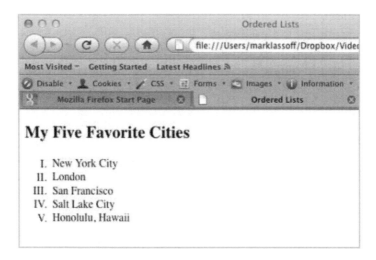

Code Listing: Ordered Lists – type'i'

```
<?xml version="1.0" encoding="UTF-8"?>
<!DOCTYPE html PUBLIC "-//W3C//DTD XHTML 1.0 Strict//EN"
"http://www.w3.org/TR/xhtml1/DTD/xhtml1-strict.dtd">
<html xmlns="http://www.w3.org/1999/xhtml" xml:lang="en" lang="en">
<head>
    <title>Ordered Lists</title>
</head>
<body>
    <h2>My Five Favorite Cities</h2>
    <ol type='i'>
        <li>New York City</li>
        <li>London</li>
        <li>San Francisco</li>
        <li>Salt Lake City</li>
        <li>Honolulu, Hawaii</li>
    </ol>
</body>
<html>
```

This is how <ol type='i'> will look when viewed in the browser:

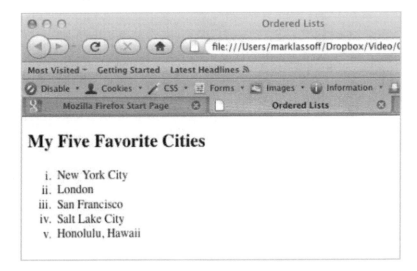

Code Listing: Ordered Lists: type='A'

```
<?xml version="1.0" encoding="UTF-8"?>
<!DOCTYPE html PUBLIC "-//W3C//DTD XHTML 1.0 Strict//EN"
"http://www.w3.org/TR/xhtml1/DTD/xhtml1-strict.dtd">
<html xmlns="http://www.w3.org/1999/xhtml" xml:lang="en" lang="en">
<head>
    <title>Ordered Lists</title>
</head>
<body>
    <h2>My Five Favorite Cities</h2>
    <ol type='A'>
        <li>New York City</li>
        <li>London</li>
        <li>San Francisco</li>
        <li>Salt Lake City</li>
        <li>Honolulu, Hawaii</li>
    </ol>
</body>
</html>
```

This is how **<ol type='A'>** will look when viewed in the browser:

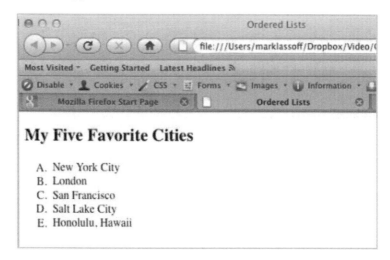

Code Listing: Ordered Lists – type='a'

```
<?xml version="1.0" encoding="UTF-8"?>
<!DOCTYPE html PUBLIC "-//W3C//DTD XHTML 1.0 Strict//EN"
"http://www.w3.org/TR/xhtml1/DTD/xhtml1-strict.dtd">
<html xmlns="http://www.w3.org/1999/xhtml" xml:lang="en" lang="en">
<head>
    <title>Ordered Lists</title>
</head>
<body>
    <h2>My Five Favorite Cities</h2>
    <ol type='a'>
        <li>New York City</li>
        <li>London</li>
        <li>San Francisco</li>
        <li>Salt Lake City</li>
        <li>Honolulu, Hawaii</li>
    </ol>
</body>
</html>
```

This is how **<ol type='a'>** will look when viewed in the browser:

Questions for Review

1. What tag do you use to begin ordered lists?
a. <bl>
b. <cl>
c. <ol>
d. <hl>

2. What tag do you put a list item under?
a. <ol>
b. <lp>
c. <lo>
d. <li>

3. What attribute and value would you use if you want your list to have uppercase letters instead of numbers?
a. <ol type='l'>
b. <ol type='i'>
c. <ol type='a'>
d. <ol type='A'>

4. What attribute and value would you use if you want your list to have uppercase Roman numerals instead of numbers?
a. <ol type='l'>
b. <ol type='i'>
c. <ol type='a'>
d. <ol type='A'>

Lab Activity

Create an HTML page that will display the following output:

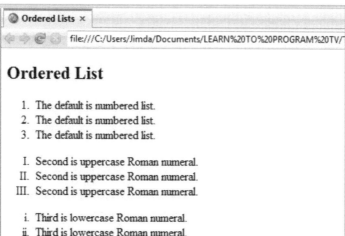

Lab Solution

```xml
<?xml version="1.0" encoding="UTF-8"?>
<!DOCTYPE html PUBLIC "-//W3C//DTD XHTML 1.0 Strict//EN"
"http://www.w3.org/TR/xhtml1/DTD/xhtml1-strict.dtd">
<html xmlns="http://www.w3.org/1999/xhtml" xml:lang="en" lang="en">
<head>
    <title>Ordered Lists</title>
</head>
<body>
    <h2>Ordered List</h2>
    <ol>
        <li>The default is numbered list.</li>
        <li>The default is numbered list.</li>
        <li>The default is numbered list.</li>
    </ol>

    <ol type='I'>
        <li>Second is uppercase Roman numeral.</li>
        <li>Second is uppercase Roman numeral.</li>
        <li>Second is uppercase Roman numeral.</li>
    </ol>

    <ol type='i'>
        <li>Third is lowercase Roman numeral.</li>
        <li>Third is lowercase Roman numeral.</li>
        <li>Third is lowercase Roman numeral.</li>
    </ol>

    <ol type='A'>
        <li>Fourth is uppercase English alphabet.</li>
        <li>Fourth is uppercase English alphabet.</li>
        <li>Fourth is uppercase English alphabet.</li>
    </ol>

    <ol type='a'>
        <li>Last is lowercase English alphabet.</li>
        <li>Last is lowercase English alphabet.</li>
        <li>Last is lowercase English alphabet.</li>
    </ol>
</body>
</html>
```

3.2 Unordered Lists

Similar to ordered lists, unordered lists allow you to display a list of items. Instead of presenting them as numbered items, list elements are displayed as bulleted lists.

Unordered lists begin with the **<ul>** tag. Each item on the list is still preceded by and completed with the **<li>** tag.

Like ordered lists, you can select the style for the list with the **'type'** attribute. The default is a solid circular bullet, but you can also use other bullet types such as square bullets or the unfilled circle. Refer to the table below to see the list of tags used to indicate the bullet type used in an unordered list.

Attribute Type for **<ul>** tag	Precedes each list type with:
<ul> (default)	Circular bullet or filled circles
<ul type="square">	Square bullet
<ul type="circles">	Circular bullet, outlined (or empty disc)
<ul type="disc">	Circular bullet or filled circles

Code Listing: Unordered List - default

```
<?xml version="1.0" encoding="UTF-8"?>
<!DOCTYPE html PUBLIC "-//W3C//DTD XHTML 1.0 Strict//EN"
"http://www.w3.org/TR/xhtml1/DTD/xhtml1-strict.dtd">
<html xmlns="http://www.w3.org/1999/xhtml" xml:lang="en" lang="en">
<head>
    <title>Unordered Lists</title>
</head>
<body>
    <h2>Some Programming Languages</h2>
    <ul>
        <li>PHP</li>
        <li>Java</li>
        <li>Javascript</li>
        <li>C++</li>
        <li>Objective C</li>
        <li>Visual Basic.net</li>
    </ul>
</body>
</html>
```

This is how a default unordered list **<ul>** looks when viewed in the browser:

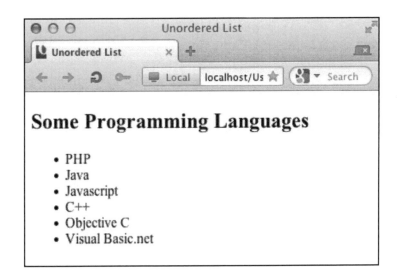

Code Listing: Unordered List - <ul type='square'>

```
<?xml version="1.0" encoding="UTF-8"?>
<!DOCTYPE html PUBLIC "-//W3C//DTD XHTML 1.0 Strict//EN"
"http://www.w3.org/TR/xhtml1/DTD/xhtml1-strict.dtd">
<html xmlns="http://www.w3.org/1999/xhtml" xml:lang="en" lang="en">
<head>
    <title>Unordered Lists</title>
</head>
<body>
    <h2>Some Programming Languages</h2>
    <ul type='square'>
        <li>PHP</li>
        <li>Java</li>
        <li>Javascript</li>
        <li>C++</li>
        <li>Objective C</li>
        <li>Visual Basic.net</li>
    </ul>
</body>
</html>
```

This is how an unordered list **<ul type='square'>** will look when viewed in the browser:

Code Listing: Unordered List - <ul type='circle'>

```
<?xml version="1.0" encoding="UTF-8"?>
<!DOCTYPE html PUBLIC "-//W3C//DTD XHTML 1.0 Strict//EN"
"http://www.w3.org/TR/xhtml1/DTD/xhtml1-strict.dtd">
<html xmlns="http://www.w3.org/1999/xhtml" xml:lang="en" lang="en">
<head>
    <title>Unordered Lists</title>
</head>
<body>
    <h2>Some Programming Languages</h2>
    <ul type='circle'>
        <li>PHP</li>
        <li>Java</li>
        <li>Javascript</li>
        <li>C++</li>
        <li>Objective C</li>
        <li>Visual Basic.net</li>
    </ul>
</body>
</html>
```

This is how an unordered list **<ul type=' circle'>** will look when viewed in the browser:

Code Listing: Unordered List - <ul type='disc'>

```
<?xml version="1.0" encoding="UTF-8"?>
<!DOCTYPE html PUBLIC "-//W3C//DTD XHTML 1.0 Strict//EN"
"http://www.w3.org/TR/xhtml1/DTD/xhtml1-strict.dtd">
<html xmlns="http://www.w3.org/1999/xhtml" xml:lang="en" lang="en">
<head>
    <title>Unordered Lists</title>
</head>
<body>
    <h2>Some Programming Languages</h2>
    <ul type='disc'>
        <li>PHP</li>
        <li>Java</li>
        <li>Javascript</li>
        <li>C++</li>
        <li>Objective C</li>
        <li>Visual Basic.net</li>
    </ul>
</body>
</html>
```

This is how **<ul type='disc'>** will look in the browser.

Questions for Review

1. What tag do unordered lists begin with?
a. <ul>
b. <ol>
c. <pl>
d. <fl>

2. What attribute and value would you use if you wanted your list to have hollow circles?
a. <ul type=prism>
b. <ul type=disc>
c. <ul type=square>
d. <ul type=circle>

3. What attribute and value would you use if you wanted your list to have filled circles?
a. <ul type=prism>
b. <ul type= disc>
c. <ul type=square>
d. <ul type=circle>

4. What attribute and value would you use if you wanted your list to have squares?
a. <ul type=prism>
b. <ul type= disc>
c. <ul type=square>
d. <ul type=circle>

Lab Activity

Create an HTML page that will display the following output:

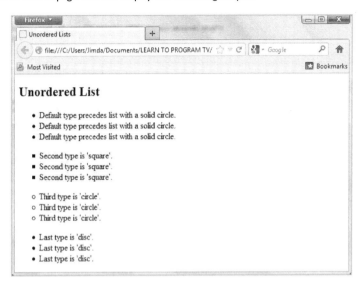

Lab Solution

```
<?xml version="1.0" encoding="UTF-8"?>
<!DOCTYPE html PUBLIC "-//W3C//DTD XHTML 1.0 Strict//EN"
"http://www.w3.org/TR/xhtml1/DTD/xhtml1-strict.dtd">
<html xmlns="http://www.w3.org/1999/xhtml" xml:lang="en" lang="en">
<head>
    <title>Unordered Lists</title>
</head>
<body>
    <h2>Unordered List</h2>
    <ul>
        <li>Default type  precedes list with a solid circle.</li>
        <li>Default type  precedes list with a solid circle.</li>
        <li>Default type  precedes list with a solid circle.</li>
    </ul>

    <ul type="square">
        <li> Second type is 'square'.</li>
        <li> Second type is 'square'.</li>
        <li> Second type is 'square'.</li>
    </ul>

    <ul type="circle">
        <li> Third type is 'circle'.</li>
        <li> Third type is 'circle'.</li>
        <li> Third type is 'circle'.</li>
    </ul>

    <ul type="disc">
        <li> Last type is 'disc'.</li>
        <li> Last type is 'disc'.</li>
        <li> Last type is 'disc'.</li>
    </ul>
</body>
</html>
```

3.3 CSS for Lists

In the previous subchapter, we styled bullet list items using HTML. Another way to adjust the look of your lists is with CSS. You will need to use the '**list-style-type**' style to change the style and appearance of the bullets. In CSS, there are several ways to introduce formatting or styling of your texts. The first thing to do is include a small CSS code block in the heading section, such as the code shown below. Both ordered and unordered lists can be styled in CSS.

```
<head>
<style type="text/css">
ul      {
list-style-type: circle;
}
</style>
</head>
```

With CSS you can also change the margin and padding of your list using the **margin** and **padding** styles. Padding allows you to add space between the content and the edge of the block containing it. Margin adds space between the content block and the next element of content on the page. This code is placed along the list style block portion in the heading as follows:

```
<head>
<style type="text/css">
ul      {
list-style-type: circle;
padding: 0px;
margin: 0px;
}
</style>
</head>
```

Many developers and designers use CSS to customize bullet graphics to improve the look of their site. Setting up a custom bullet is easy. We do this by including the list item selector (li) inside the style code block and pulling in a bullet graphic image file. In this example we are using 'star.png' as the image.

To add the image, use the **li** selector and change the background style by using the '**background-image**' attribute and indicating the path of the file name. You also want to set the **background-repeat** style to 'no repeat' so that the image does not appear more than once on each line.

Refer to the following code to see how these steps come together in the unordered list (ul) code block:

```
<head>
<style type="text/css">
ul      {
list-style-type: circle;
padding: 0px;
margin: 0px;
}
        li      {
```

```
background-image: url(star.png);
background-repeat: no-repeat;
                              }
</style>
</head>
```

Finally, it's important to change the position of the custom bullet so it doesn't overlap the text. You can do this by using the **background-position** attribute and **padding-left attribute**. However, you must change your pixel values to work with your custom bullet.

```
<head>
<style type="text/css">
ul      {
list-style-type: circle;
padding: 0px;
margin: 0px;
}
li      {
background-image: url(star.png);
background-repeat: no-repeat;
background-position: 3px 1px;
padding-left: 20px;
                              }
</style>
</head>
```

The complete code set is as follows:

Code Listing: Unordered Lists

```
<?xml version="1.0" encoding="UTF-8"?>
<!DOCTYPE html PUBLIC "-//W3C//DTD XHTML 1.0 Strict//EN"
"http://www.w3.org/TR/xhtml1/DTD/xhtml1-strict.dtd">
<html xmlns="http://www.w3.org/1999/xhtml" xml:lang="en" lang="en">
<head>
    <title>Unordered Lists</title>
    <style type="text/css">
        ul      {
                    list-style-type: none;
                    padding: 0px;
                    margin: 0px;
                }

        li      {

                    background-image: url(star.png);
                    background-repeat: no-repeat;
                    background-position: 3px 1px;
                    padding-left: 20px;
                }
    </style>
</head>
<body>
    <h2>Some Programming Languages</h2>
    <ul type="disc">
        <li>PHP</li>
        <li>Java</li>
        <li>Javascript</li>
        <li>C++</li>
        <li>Objective C</li>
        <li>Visual Basic.net</li>
    </ul>
</body>
</html>
```

This is how custom button styling will appear in the browser:

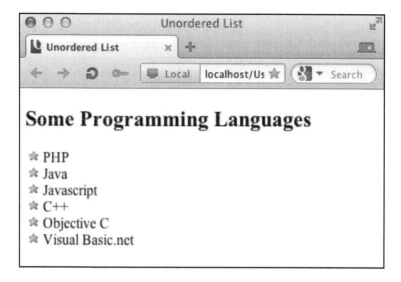

Questions for Review

1. What style in CSS should you use to determine the style of the list?
a. list-style-type:
b. list-type:
c. list-style:
d. list-set-style:

2. If you want to create a custom button using a png file, what CSS attribute will you need?
a. background-png; url
b. background-image; url (name.png)
c. background-image; (name.png)
d. background; (name.png)

Chapter 3 Lab Exercises

1) Create a correct and standard-compliant XHTML basic document structure. Inside the **<title>** element, place the text **Lab 3: Lists**.

2) Include an **<h2>** element just below the opening body tag in your script. Between the opening and closing heading tag, insert the text "**Ten Technology Companies**" followed by an **ordered list** that contains the names of the following 10 companies:

Dell	Apple	HP
Facebook	Google	Motorola
LinkedIn	Amazon	StumbleUpon
Adobe		

3) Below the code for the ordered list, insert another **<h2>** element and use the text "**US-Based Airlines**" as the element text. Add an **unordered list** and list the names of the following airlines:

American	United
US Airways	Delta
Southwest	Frontier
JetBlue	Hawaiian Air
Alaska Air	Virgin America

4) Using the procedure presented, alter the CSS for the unordered list to use a custom bullet. You may create your own bullet graphics and use them in completing this exercise.

Your output should appear similar to this:

Ten Technology Companies

1. Dell
2. Facebook
3. LinkedIn
4. Adobe
5. Apple
6. Google
7. Amazon
8. HP
9. Motorola
10. StumbleUpon

US-Based Airlines

- American
- US Airways
- Southwest
- JetBlue
- Alaska Air
- United
- Delta
- Frontier
- Hawaiian Air
- Virgin America

Lab Solution

```
<?xml version="1.0" encoding="UTF-8"?>
<!DOCTYPE html PUBLIC "-//W3C//DTD XHTML 1.0 Strict//EN"
"http://www.w3.org/TR/xhtml1/DTD/xhtml1-strict.dtd">
<html xmlns="http://www.w3.org/1999/xhtml" xml:lang="en" lang="en">
<head>
    <title>Lab 3: Lists</title>

</head>
<body>
    <h2>Ten Technology Companies</h2>
    <ol>
        <li>Dell</li>
        <li>Facebook</li>
        <li>LinkedIn</li>
        <li>Adobe</li>
        <li>Apple</li>
        <li>Google</li>
        <li>Amazon</li>
        <li>HP</li>
        <li>Motorola</li>
        <li>StumbleUpon</li>
    </ol>
    <h2>US-Based Airlines</h2>
    <style type="text/css">
        ul      {
                    list-style-type: none;
                    padding: 0px;
                    margin: 0px;

                }

        ul li   {
                    background-image: url(star-bullet.png);
                    background-repeat: no-repeat;
                    background-position: 3px 1px;
                    padding-left: 20px;

                }
    </style>
    <ul>
        <li>American</li>
        <li>US Airways</li>
        <li>Southwest</li>
        <li>JetBlue</li>
        <li>Alaska Air</li>
        <li>United</li>
        <li>Delta</li>
        <li>Frontier</li>
        <li>Hawaiian Air</li>
        <li>Virgin America</li>
    </ul>

</body>
</html>
```

Chapter 3 Summary

In this chapter, you learned about HTML and CSS styling for **ordered** and **unordered lists** and **how to set up a custom-made bullet graphic**.

Chapter 4: Creating HTML Links

Chapter Objectives:
•Students will be able to create internal and external HTML links.
•Students will be able to implement anchor links that help users navigate a webpage.
•Students will be able to style links using CSS.

4.1 Creating External and Internal Links

In this section, we are going to discuss links which are sometimes referred to as hyperlinks, a term coined by Apple Computers and implemented in the 1980s in their HyperCard software.

Links are what allow users to move from one document page or section to another in HTML. There are different types of links. In this subchapter, we will cover external and internal links.

External links allow users to move from one site to another while on the internet. To create a link, you use the anchor tag **<a>** together with the attribute **href**, which stands for hypertext reference. When creating an external link, you begin with **<a,** followed by **href=**, then by the URL you are linking to, enclosed in double quotes. End the element with an angle bracket. This precedes the text in the document you want to create the link in. Close the link tag with **</a>**. Collectively:

```
<a href= "http://www.url.extension name">link text</a>
```

Here are examples of external links. Some are contained inside a paragraph tag:

```
<a href="http://www.yahoo.com">Yahoo!</a>
```

```
<p>I get my news from <a href="http://www.cnn.com>CNN</a></p>
```

```
<p>Fly <a href=http://www.jetblue.com>jetBlue</a></p>
```

Internal links are written in a similar fashion to external links. Internal links direct the user to another page within the same website or domain. If the HTML document you want to link to is located in the same folder as the original document, you simply indicate the name of the file in the link. For example, if you have a file named "links.html" you would link it as:

```
<a href="links.html">My Links</a>
```

However, if you have a file in a different folder, make sure you add the path to the link by typing the folder name, followed by the forward slash '/' and finally the HTML document name. For example, if your file is named "links.html" and is inside a folder named "files", you will have your code as:

```
<a href="files/links.html">My Links</a>
```

This will direct you to a folder named "file" that contains the file "links.html".

Now, if you need to go up one level/folder higher, precede the link with:

```
' ../ '
```

Let us say you have a main page **home.html** and **links.html** as its second page. From home.html you navigated away to its second page. Now you want to go back to **home.html** from **links.html**, your code must now include:

```
<a href="../home.html">Go home</a>
```

Refer to the code below showing the use of an external link.

Notice that the bottom link (internal link) does not function yet, but the three external links do.

Code Listing: Creating Links

```
<?xml version="1.0" encoding="UTF-8"?>
<!DOCTYPE html PUBLIC "-//W3C//DTD XHTML 1.0 Strict//EN"
"http://www.w3.org/TR/xhtml1/DTD/xhtml1-strict.dtd">
<html xmlns="http://www.w3.org/1999/xhtml" xml:lang="en" lang="en">
<head>
    <title>Creating Links</title>
</head>
<body>
    <p><a
href="http://www.learntoprogram.tv">LearnToProgram.tv</a></p>
    <p>I watch <a href="http://www.cnn.com">CNN</a> for political
reporting</p>
    <p><a href="http://www.msnbc.com">MsNbc</a></p>
    <p><a href="details_pages/places.html">Places I'd like to
visit</a></p>
</body>
</html>
```

This is what the page will look like when viewed in the browser:

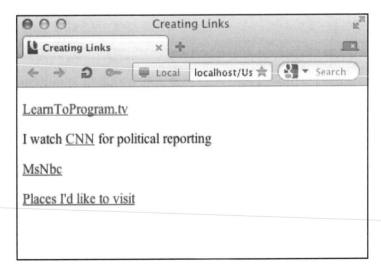

Now, for the internal link "Places I'd like to visit" in the above example work, a separate HTML file named **places.html**, contained in a folder named **details_pages** must exist. Create a folder now named details_pages. Copy the code below in a file named places.html and save it in the folder you just created. Creating this file will ensure that the internal link "Places I'd like to visit" works.

Code Listing: Internal Links

```
<?xml version="1.0" encoding="UTF-8"?>
<!DOCTYPE html PUBLIC "-//W3C//DTD XHTML 1.0 Strict//EN"
"http://www.w3.org/TR/xhtml1/DTD/xhtml1-strict.dtd">
<html xmlns="http://www.w3.org/1999/xhtml" xml:lang="en" lang="en">
<head>
    <title>Places I'd like to Go</title>
</head>
<body>
    <ul>
        <li>Aspen, Co</li>
        <li>Monaco</li>
        <li>Spain</li>
        <li>Dubai</li>
    </ul>
    <a href="../links.html">Go Back</a>
</body>
</html>
```

Included at the bottom of this code is the instruction to "Go back" to the main page. The "../" preceding the file **links.html** directs the link pointer to move up a folder level to locate the page.

This is what the page will look like when viewed in the browser:

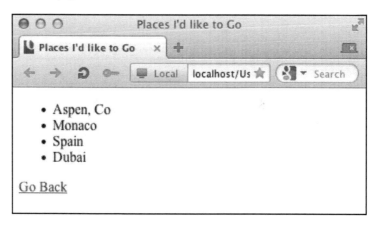

If you encountered an error message, make sure you have the following:
      -a complete and correct pathname for the folder that contains the HTML pages
      -correct filenames of your HTML pages

Take extra care with the folder and filename links, as the browser will give an error message if it does not find the path and filename indicated in the code/link.

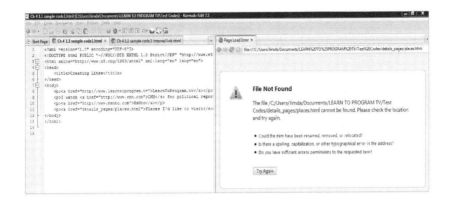

Questions for Review

1. Which among the following is the anchor tag?

a. `<a>`
b. `<anchor>`
c. `<b>`
d. `<link>`

2. If you want your link, www.famewebsite.com, in the text "Link", which anchor tag would be correct?

a. `<a href= "http://famewebsite.com" Link>`
b. `<a href= "http://famewebsite.com"> </a> Link`
c. `<a href= "http://famewebsite.com"> Link </a>`
d. `<a href="http://fakewebsite.com/Link" </a>`

3. If you want to link internally to a page named "new.html", which tag would you use?

a. `<a href= http://www.yourwebsite.com/new.html`
b. `<a href= "http://www.yourwebsite.com/main/new.html""> </a>`
c. `<a href= new.html> Link </a>`
d. `<a href="new.html">`

4. You need to create an internal link to a page named "new.html", found in a separate folder named "folder". How should your link be coded?

a. `<a href= "http://www.yourwebsite.com/new.html">`
b. `<a href= "folder/new.html">`
c. `<a href= "//folder/new.html">`
d. `<a href="/folder/new.html">`

4.2 Creating Page Anchors

Page Anchors are links where both the link text and the link destination are on the same page, allowing navigation within the page.

Long web pages frequently use page anchors to help users easily navigate within the page rather than scrolling over the entire page to browse the full page content. To make navigation possible, two anchor attributes are used in combination:

- the hypertext reference attribute **<a href=** attribute associated with the link text
- and name attribute **<a name=** attribute associated with the link destination

Here is the syntax for both page anchor elements when used:

```
<a href="#anchor name">link text</a>

 <a name="anchor name"/>link destination</a>
```

Here is a list of the page anchors and corresponding links:

```
<a name="top"/>

<a href="#Believing">Don't Stop Believing</a>
<a name="Believing"/>Don't Stop Believing...</a>

<a href="#killer">A Killer Smile</a>
<a name="killer"/>A Killer Smile</a>

<a href="#people">Meeting the Right People</a>
<a name="people"/> Meeting the Right People </a>

<a href="#time">Putting in the Time</a>
<a name="time"/> Putting in the Time </a>

<a href="#success">Creating Your Own Success</a>
<a name="success"/> Creating Your Own Success </a>

<a href="#Believing">Don't Stop Believing</a>
```

Shown next is the complete code example for this chapter.

Code Listing: Anchor Links

```
<?xml version="1.0" encoding="UTF-8"?>
<!DOCTYPE html PUBLIC "-//W3C//DTD XHTML 1.0 Strict//EN"
"http://www.w3.org/TR/xhtml1/DTD/xhtml1-strict.dtd">
<html xmlns="http://www.w3.org/1999/xhtml" xml:lang="en" lang="en">
<head>
    <title>Page Anchors</title>
    <style type="text/css">
        h2  {
            font-family: Georgia, serif;
            font-size: 1.75em;
        }
```

```
            p   {
                 font-family: Helvetica, Arial, sans-serif;
                 font-size: .8em;
            }
        </style>
</head>
<body>
    <div>
        <a name="top"/>
        <p><a href="#Believing">Don't Stop Believing...</a><br/>
            <a href="#killer">A Killer Smile</a><br/>
            <a href="#people">Meeting the Right People</a><br/>
            <a href="#time">Putting in the Time</a><br/>
            <a href="#success">Creating Your Own Success</a><br/>
    </div>
    <div>
        <h2><a name="Believing" />Don't Stop Believing...</h2>
        <p>Lorem ipsum dolor sit amet, consectetur adipiscing elit.
Phasellus sagittis justo ac neque scelerisque venenatis. Vestibulum
sit amet enim leo, sed suscipit velit. Maecenas vel ipsum arcu, sit
amet lobortis nisi. Vivamus luctus ipsum aliquam mi aliquet
tincidunt. Nam eleifend hendrerit consectetur. Praesent sed massa
quis arcu malesuada ornare. Quisque non odio quis ante porttitor
vestibulum.</p>

<p>In hac habitasse platea dictumst. Suspendisposuere vehicula
libero in varius. Suspendisse potenti. Mauris sit amet odio in
felis varius accumsan. In vitae sem ipsum. Fusce faucibus sem id
ligula ornare posuere vehicula elit porta. Ut ac est felis. Sed et
imperdiet nisl. Donec nec imperdiet enim. Sed metus nisl, rutrum in
interdum at, elementum eu elit. Vivamus non sapien nec dui
vestibulum suscipit nec vel metus. Suspendisse potenti. Proin
pellentesque, dui eget congue elementum, ante purus pharetra metus,
eget bibendum lacus neque lacinia est. Morbi rutrum diam sit amet
tellus faucibus egestas. Sed quam lectus, adipiscing eget placerat
in, laoreet eget ipsum.</p>

<p>Vestibulum viverra, velit non molestie ultrices, dolor nibh
vulputate erat, quis luctus ligula sem eu lacus. Nunc ullamcorper,
nibh in iaculis gravida, arcu justo luctus neque, ut laoreet erat
lorem vitae erat. Sed dapibus ligula tempus augue ultricies dictum.
Morbi scelerisque nisi fringilla sem ultricies imperdiet. Lorem
ipsum dolor sit amet, consectetur adipiscing elit. Class aptent
taciti sociosqu ad litora torquent per conubia nostra, per inceptos
himenaeos. Nunc sagittis vestibulum est, non pulvinar tellus
convallis nec. Duis sit amet ligula eu ante vehicula laoreet id sed
odio. Aliquam erat volutpat. Proin nisl augue, hendrerit in porta
in, mattis egestas orci. Cras vel aliquet quam. Aenean gravida,
odio et ullamcorper tincidunt, neque est fringilla mi, vel commodo
risus augue non felis.</p>
    </div>

    <div>
        <h2><a name="killer"/>A Killer Smile...</h2>
        <p>Lorem ipsum dolor sit amet, consectetur adipiscing elit.
Phasellus sagittis justo ac neque scelerisque venenatis. Vestibulum
sit amet enim leo, sed suscipit velit. Maecenas vel ipsum arcu, sit
amet lobortis nisi. Vivamus luctus ipsum aliquam mi aliquet
tincidunt. Nam eleifend hendrerit consectetur. Praesent sed massa
```

quis arcu malesuada ornare. Quisque non odio quis ante porttitor
vestibulum.</p>

<p>In hac habitasse platea dictumst. Suspendisse posuere vehicula
libero in varius. Suspendisse potenti. Mauris sit amet odio in
felis varius accumsan. In vitae sem ipsum. Fusce faucibus sem id
ligula ornare posuere vehicula elit porta. Ut ac est felis. Sed et
imperdiet nisl. Donec nec imperdiet enim. Sed metus nisl, rutrum in
interdum at, elementum eu elit. Vivamus non sapien nec dui
vestibulum suscipit nec vel metus. Suspendisse potenti. Proin
pellentesque, dui eget congue elementum, ante purus pharetra metus,
eget bibendum lacus neque lacinia est. Morbi rutrum diam sit amet
tellus faucibus egestas. Sed quam lectus, adipiscing eget placerat
in, laoreet eget ipsum.</p>

<p>Vestibulum viverra, velit non molestie ultrices, dolor nibh
vulputate erat, quis luctus ligula sem eu lacus. Nunc ullamcorper,
nibh in iaculis gravida, arcu justo luctus neque, ut laoreet erat
lorem vitae erat. Sed dapibus ligula tempus augue ultricies dictum.
Morbi scelerisque nisi fringilla sem ultricies imperdiet. Lorem
ipsum dolor sit amet, consectetur adipiscing elit. Class aptent
taciti sociosqu ad litora torquent per conubia nostra, per inceptos
himenaeos. Nunc sagittis vestibulum est, non pulvinar tellus
convallis nec. Duis sit amet ligula eu ante vehicula laoreet id sed
odio. Aliquam erat volutpat. Proin nisl augue, hendrerit in porta
in, mattis egestas orci. Cras vel aliquet quam. Aenean gravida,
odio et ullamcorper tincidunt, neque est fringilla mi, vel commodo
risus augue non felis.</p>
    </div>

    <div>
        <h2><a name="people"/>Meeting The Right People...</h2>
        <p>Lorem ipsum dolor sit amet, consectetur adipiscing elit.
Phasellus sagittis justo ac neque scelerisque venenatis. Vestibulum
sit amet enim leo, sed suscipit velit. Maecenas vel ipsum arcu, sit
amet lobortis nisi. Vivamus luctus ipsum aliquam mi aliquet
tincidunt. Nam eleifend hendrerit consectetur. Praesent sed massa
quis arcu malesuada ornare. Quisque non odio quis ante porttitor
vestibulum.</p>

<p>In hac habitasse platea dictumst. Suspendisse posuere vehicula
libero in varius. Suspendisse potenti. Mauris sit amet odio in
felis varius accumsan. In vitae sem ipsum. Fusce faucibus sem id
ligula ornare posuere vehicula elit porta. Ut ac est felis. Sed et
imperdiet nisl. Donec nec imperdiet enim. Sed metus nisl, rutrum in
interdum at, elementum eu elit. Vivamus non sapien nec dui
vestibulum suscipit nec vel metus. Suspendisse potenti. Proin
pellentesque, dui eget congue elementum, ante purus pharetra metus,
eget bibendum lacus neque lacinia est. Morbi rutrum diam sit amet
tellus faucibus egestas. Sed quam lectus, adipiscing eget placerat
in, laoreet eget ipsum.</p>

<p>Vestibulum viverra, velit non molestie ultrices, dolor nibh
vulputate erat, quis luctus ligula sem eu lacus. Nunc ullamcorper,
nibh in iaculis gravida, arcu justo luctus neque, ut laoreet erat
lorem vitae erat. Sed dapibus ligula tempus augue ultricies dictum.
Morbi scelerisque nisi fringilla sem ultricies imperdiet. Lorem
ipsum dolor sit amet, consectetur adipiscing elit. Class aptent
taciti sociosqu ad litora torquent per conubia nostra, per inceptos
himenaeos. Nunc sagittis vestibulum est, non pulvinar tellus

convallis nec. Duis sit amet ligula eu ante vehicula laoreet id sed
odio. Aliquam erat volutpat. Proin nisl augue, hendrerit in porta
in, mattis egestas orci. Cras vel aliquet quam. Aenean gravida,
odio et ullamcorper tincidunt, neque est fringilla mi, vel commodo
risus augue non felis.</p>
    </div>

    <div>
        <h2><a name="time"/>Puting in the Time...</h2>
        <p>Lorem ipsum dolor sit amet, consectetur adipiscing elit.
Phasellus sagittis justo ac neque scelerisque venenatis. Vestibulum
sit amet enim leo, sed suscipit velit. Maecenas vel ipsum arcu, sit
amet lobortis nisi. Vivamus luctus ipsum aliquam mi aliquet
tincidunt. Nam eleifend hendrerit consectetur. Praesent sed massa
quis arcu malesuada ornare. Quisque non odio quis ante porttitor
vestibulum.</p>

<p>In hac habitasse platea dictumst. Suspendisse posuere vehicula
libero in varius. Suspendisse potenti. Mauris sit amet odio in
felis varius accumsan. In vitae sem ipsum. Fusce faucibus sem id
ligula ornare posuere vehicula elit porta. Ut ac est felis. Sed et
imperdiet nisl. Donec nec imperdiet enim. Sed metus nisl, rutrum in
interdum at, elementum eu elit. Vivamus non sapien nec dui
vestibulum suscipit nec vel metus. Suspendisse potenti. Proin
pellentesque, dui eget congue elementum, ante purus pharetra metus,
eget bibendum lacus neque lacinia est. Morbi rutrum diam sit amet
tellus faucibus egestas. Sed quam lectus, adipiscing eget placerat
in, laoreet eget ipsum.</p>

<p>Vestibulum viverra, velit non molestie ultrices, dolor nibh
vulputate erat, quis luctus ligula sem eu lacus. Nunc ullamcorper,
nibh in iaculis gravida, arcu justo luctus neque, ut laoreet erat
lorem vitae erat. Sed dapibus ligula tempus augue ultricies dictum.
Morbi scelerisque nisi fringilla sem ultricies imperdiet. Lorem
ipsum dolor sit amet, consectetur adipiscing elit. Class aptent
taciti sociosqu ad litora torquent per conubia nostra, per inceptos
himenaeos. Nunc sagittis vestibulum est, non pulvinar tellus
convallis nec. Duis sit amet ligula eu ante vehicula laoreet id sed
odio. Aliquam erat volutpat. Proin nisl augue, hendrerit in porta
in, mattis egestas orci. Cras vel aliquet quam. Aenean gravida,
odio et ullamcorper tincidunt, neque est fringilla mi, vel commodo
risus augue non felis.</p>
    </div>

    <div>
        <h2><a name="success"/>Creating Your Own Success...</h2>
        <p>Lorem ipsum dolor sit amet, consectetur adipiscing elit.
Phasellus sagittis justo ac neque scelerisque venenatis. Vestibulum
sit amet enim leo, sed suscipit velit. Maecenas vel ipsum arcu, sit
amet lobortis nisi. Vivamus luctus ipsum aliquam mi aliquet
tincidunt. Nam eleifend hendrerit consectetur. Praesent sed massa
quis arcu malesuada ornare. Quisque non odio quis ante porttitor
vestibulum.</p>

<p>In hac habitasse platea dictumst. Suspendisse posuere vehicula
libero in varius. Suspendisse potenti. Mauris sit amet odio in
felis varius accumsan. In vitae sem ipsum. Fusce faucibus sem id
ligula ornare posuere vehicula elit porta. Ut ac est felis. Sed et
imperdiet nisl. Donec nec imperdiet enim. Sed metus nisl, rutrum in
interdum at, elementum eu elit. Vivamus non sapien nec dui

vestibulum suscipit nec vel metus. Suspendisse potenti. Proin
pellentesque, dui eget congue elementum, ante purus pharetra metus,
eget bibendum lacus neque lacinia est. Morbi rutrum diam sit amet
tellus faucibus egestas. Sed quam lectus, adipiscing eget placerat
in, laoreet eget ipsum.<p>

<p>Vestibulum viverra, velit non molestie ultrices, dolor nibh
vulputate erat, quis luctus ligula sem eu lacus. Nunc ullamcorper,
nibh in iaculis gravida, arcu justo luctus neque, ut laoreet erat
lorem vitae erat. Sed dapibus ligula tempus augue ultricies dictum.
Morbi scelerisque nisi fringilla sem ultricies imperdiet. Lorem
ipsum dolor sit amet, consectetur adipiscing elit. Class aptent
taciti sociosqu ad litora torquent per conubia nostra, per inceptos
himenaeos. Nunc sagittis vestibulum est, non pulvinar tellus
convallis nec. Duis sit amet ligula eu ante vehicula laoreet id sed
odio. Aliquam erat volutpat. Proin nisl augue, hendrerit in porta
in, mattis egestas orci. Cras vel aliquet quam. Aenean gravida,
odio et ullamcorper tincidunt, neque est fringilla mi, vel commodo
risus augue non felis.</p>
    </div>
    <a href="#top">Top</a>
</body>
</html>

Notice other name anchors used in the example:

<a name="Top"/>

and

<a href="#top">Top<a/>

These allowed the user to immediately navigate at the page's top location.

4.3 Styling Links with CSS Pseudo-Classes

Styling links with CSS Pseudo-class is slightly different than styling other elements. This is because pseudo-class anchors have different states. Pseudo-selectors match each of the link states.

There are three link states and each has its own pseudo selector:

State	Pseudo-class Selector
plain link	a:link
link that has been visited	a:visited
user hovering over the link	a:hover

In this example shown, the link is made red, the font bold, and not underlined. The CSS code is as follows:

```
<style type="text/css">
        h2      {
                font-family: Georgia, serif;
                font-size: 1.75em;
                }
        p       {
font-family: Helvetica, Arial, sans-serif;
                font-size: .8em;
}
a:link, a:visited{
color:   red;
font-weight:  bold;
text-decoration:  none;
}
a: hover{
color:   red;
font-weight:   bold;
text-decoration:  underline;
                }
                </style>
```

a:link and **a: visited** have been combined since they share the same style and value, although encoding them as separate classes is syntactically correct and will render the same effect—displaying the same style and value.

Code Listing: CSS for Links

```
<?xml version="1.0" encoding="UTF-8"?>
<!DOCTYPE html PUBLIC "-//W3C//DTD XHTML 1.0 Strict//EN"
"http://www.w3.org/TR/xhtml1/DTD/xhtml1-strict.dtd">
<html xmlns="http://www.w3.org/1999/xhtml" xml:lang="en" lang="en">
<head>
    <title>Page Anchors</title>
    <style type="text/css">
        h2   {
            font-family: Georgia, serif;
```

```
                font-size: 1.75em;
                }

        p    {
                font-family: Helvetica, Arial, sans-serif;
                font-size: .8em;
                }
            a:link, a:visited{
                color: red;
                font-weight: bold;
                text-decoration: none;
                }
            a:hover{
                color: red;
                font-weight: bold;
                text-decoration: underline;
                }
        }
    </style>
</head>
<body>
    <div>
        <a name="top"/>
        <p><a href="#Believing">Don't Stop Believing...</a><br/>
            <a href="#killer">A Killer Smile</a><br/>
            <a href="#people">Meeting The Right People</a><br/>
            <a href="#time">Putting In the Time</a><br/>
            <a href="#success">Creating Your Own Success</a><br/>
        </div>
        <div>
            <h2><a name="Believing" />Don't Stop Believing...</h2>
            <p>Lorem ipsum dolor sit amet, consectetur adipiscing elit.
Phasellus sagittis justo ac neque scelerisque venenatis. Vestibulum
sit amet enim leo, sed suscipit velit. Maecenas vel ipsum arcu, sit
amet lobortis nisi. Vivamus luctus ipsum aliquam mi aliquet
tincidunt. Nam eleifend hendrerit consectetur. Praesent sed massa
quis arcu malesuada ornare. Quisque non odio quis ante porttitor
vestibulum.</p>

<p>In hac habitasse platea dictumst. Suspendisse posuere vehicula
libero in varius. Suspendisse potenti. Mauris sit amet odio in
felis varius accumsan. In vitae sem ipsum. Fusce faucibus sem id
ligula ornare posuere vehicula elit porta. Ut ac est felis. Sed et
imperdiet nisl. Donec nec imperdiet enim. Sed metus nisl, rutrum in
interdum at, elementum eu elit. Vivamus non sapien nec dui
vestibulum suscipit nec vel metus. Suspendisse potenti. Proin
pellentesque, dui eget congue elementum, ante purus pharetra metus,
eget bibendum lacus neque lacinia est. Morbi rutrum diam sit amet
tellus faucibus egestas. Sed quam lectus, adipiscing eget placerat
in, laoreet eget ipsum.</p>

<p>Vestibulum viverra, velit non molestie ultrices, dolor nibh
vulputate erat, quis luctus ligula sem eu lacus. Nunc ullamcorper,
nibh in iaculis gravida, arcu justo luctus neque, ut laoreet erat
lorem vitae erat. Sed dapibus ligula tempus augue ultricies dictum.
Morbi scelerisque nisi fringilla sem ultricies imperdiet. Lorem
ipsum dolor sit amet, consectetur adipiscing elit. Class aptent
taciti sociosqu ad litora torquent per conubia nostra, per inceptos
himenaeos. Nunc sagittis vestibulum est, non pulvinar tellus
convallis nec. Duis sit amet ligula eu ante vehicula laoreet id sed
odio. Aliquam erat volutpat. Proin nisl augue, hendrerit in porta
```

in, mattis egestas orci. Cras vel aliquet quam. Aenean gravida,
odio et ullamcorper tincidunt, neque est fringilla mi, vel commodo
risus augue non felis.</p>
    </div>

    <div>
        <h2><a name="killer"/>A Killer Smile...</h2>
        <p>Lorem ipsum dolor sit amet, consectetur adipiscing elit.
Phasellus sagittis justo ac neque scelerisque venenatis. Vestibulum
sit amet enim leo, sed suscipit velit. Maecenas vel ipsum arcu, sit
amet lobortis nisi. Vivamus luctus ipsum aliquam mi aliquet
tincidunt. Nam eleifend hendrerit consectetur. Praesent sed massa
quis arcu malesuada ornare. Quisque non odio quis ante porttitor
vestibulum.</p>

<p>In hac habitasse platea dictumst. Suspendisse posuere vehicula
libero in varius. Suspendisse potenti. Mauris sit amet odio in
felis varius accumsan. In vitae sem ipsum. Fusce faucibus sem id
ligula ornare posuere vehicula elit porta. Ut ac est felis. Sed et
imperdiet nisl. Donec nec imperdiet enim. Sed metus nisl, rutrum in
interdum at, elementum eu elit. Vivamus non sapien nec dui
vestibulum suscipit nec vel metus. Suspendisse potenti. Proin
pellentesque, dui eget congue elementum, ante purus pharetra metus,
eget bibendum lacus neque lacinia est. Morbi rutrum diam sit amet
tellus faucibus egestas. Sed quam lectus, adipiscing eget placerat
in, laoreet eget ipsum.</p>

<p>Vestibulum viverra, velit non molestie ultrices, dolor nibh
vulputate erat, quis luctus ligula sem eu lacus. Nunc ullamcorper,
nibh in iaculis gravida, arcu justo luctus neque, ut laoreet erat
lorem vitae erat. Sed dapibus ligula tempus augue ultricies dictum.
Morbi scelerisque nisi fringilla sem ultricies imperdiet. Lorem
ipsum dolor sit amet, consectetur adipiscing elit. Class aptent
taciti sociosqu ad litora torquent per conubia nostra, per inceptos
himenaeos. Nunc sagittis vestibulum est, non pulvinar tellus
convallis nec. Duis sit amet ligula eu ante vehicula laoreet id sed
odio. Aliquam erat volutpat. Proin nisl augue, hendrerit in porta
in, mattis egestas orci. Cras vel aliquet quam. Aenean gravida,
odio et ullamcorper tincidunt, neque est fringilla mi, vel commodo
risus augue non felis.</p>
    </div>

    <div>
        <h2><a name="people"/>Meeting The Right People...</h2>
        <p>Lorem ipsum dolor sit amet, consectetur adipiscing elit.
Phasellus sagittis justo ac neque scelerisque venenatis. Vestibulum
sit amet enim leo, sed suscipit velit. Maecenas vel ipsum arcu, sit
amet lobortis nisi. Vivamus luctus ipsum aliquam mi aliquet
tincidunt. Nam eleifend hendrerit consectetur. Praesent sed massa
quis arcu malesuada ornare. Quisque non odio quis ante porttitor
vestibulum.</p>

<p>In hac habitasse platea dictumst. Suspendisse posuere vehicula
libero in varius. Suspendisse potenti. Mauris sit amet odio in
felis varius accumsan. In vitae sem ipsum. Fusce faucibus sem id
ligula ornare posuere vehicula elit porta. Ut ac est felis. Sed et
imperdiet nisl. Donec nec imperdiet enim. Sed metus nisl, rutrum in
interdum at, elementum eu elit. Vivamus non sapien nec dui
vestibulum suscipit nec vel metus. Suspendisse potenti. Proin
pellentesque, dui eget congue elementum, ante purus pharetra metus,

eget bibendum lacus neque lacinia est. Morbi rutrum diam sit amet
tellus faucibus egestas. Sed quam lectus, adipiscing eget placerat
in, laoreet eget ipsum.</p>

<p>Vestibulum viverra, velit non molestie ultrices, dolor nibh
vulputate erat, quis luctus ligula sem eu lacus. Nunc ullamcorper,
nibh in iaculis gravida, arcu justo luctus neque, ut laoreet erat
lorem vitae erat. Sed dapibus ligula tempus augue ultricies dictum.
Morbi scelerisque nisi fringilla sem ultricies imperdiet. Lorem
ipsum dolor sit amet, consectetur adipiscing elit. Class aptent
taciti sociosqu ad litora torquent per conubia nostra, per inceptos
himenaeos. Nunc sagittis vestibulum est, non pulvinar tellus
convallis nec. Duis sit amet ligula eu ante vehicula laoreet id sed
odio. Aliquam erat volutpat. Proin nisl augue, hendrerit in porta
in, mattis egestas orci. Cras vel aliquet quam. Aenean gravida,
odio et ullamcorper tincidunt, neque est fringilla mi, vel commodo
risus augue non felis.</p>
    </div>

    <div>
        <h2><a name="time"/>Puting in the Time...</h2>
        <p>Lorem ipsum dolor sit amet, consectetur adipiscing elit.
Phasellus sagittis justo ac neque scelerisque venenatis. Vestibulum
sit amet enim leo, sed suscipit velit. Maecenas vel ipsum arcu, sit
amet lobortis nisi. Vivamus luctus ipsum aliquam mi aliquet
tincidunt. Nam eleifend hendrerit consectetur. Praesent sed massa
quis arcu malesuada ornare. Quisque non odio quis ante porttitor
vestibulum.</p>

<p>In hac habitasse platea dictumst. Suspendisse posuere vehicula
libero in varius. Suspendisse potenti. Mauris sit amet odio in
felis varius accumsan. In vitae sem ipsum. Fusce faucibus sem id
ligula ornare posuere vehicula elit porta. Ut ac est felis. Sed et
imperdiet nisl. Donec nec imperdiet enim. Sed metus nisl, rutrum in
interdum at, elementum eu elit. Vivamus non sapien nec dui
vestibulum suscipit nec vel metus. Suspendisse potenti. Proin
pellentesque, dui eget congue elementum, ante purus pharetra metus,
eget bibendum lacus neque lacinia est. Morbi rutrum diam sit amet
tellus faucibus egestas. Sed quam lectus, adipiscing eget placerat
in, laoreet eget ipsum.</p>

<p>Vestibulum viverra, velit non molestie ultrices, dolor nibh
vulputate erat, quis luctus ligula sem eu lacus. Nunc ullamcorper,
nibh in iaculis gravida, arcu justo luctus neque, ut laoreet erat
lorem vitae erat. Sed dapibus ligula tempus augue ultricies dictum.
Morbi scelerisque nisi fringilla sem ultricies imperdiet. Lorem
ipsum dolor sit amet, consectetur adipiscing elit. Class aptent
taciti sociosqu ad litora torquent per conubia nostra, per inceptos
himenaeos. Nunc sagittis vestibulum est, non pulvinar tellus
convallis nec. Duis sit amet ligula eu ante vehicula laoreet id sed
odio. Aliquam erat volutpat. Proin nisl augue, hendrerit in porta
in, mattis egestas orci. Cras vel aliquet quam. Aenean gravida,
odio et ullamcorper tincidunt, neque est fringilla mi, vel commodo
risus augue non felis.</p>
    </div>

    <div>
        <h2><a name="success"/>Creating Your Own Success...</h2>
        <p>Lorem ipsum dolor sit amet, consectetur adipiscing elit.
Phasellus sagittis justo ac neque scelerisque venenatis. Vestibulum

sit amet enim leo, sed suscipit velit. Maecenas vel ipsum arcu, sit
amet lobortis nisi. Vivamus luctus ipsum aliquam mi aliquet
tincidunt. Nam eleifend hendrerit consectetur. Praesent sed massa
quis arcu malesuada ornare. Quisque non odio quis ante porttitor
vestibulum.</p>

<p>In hac habitasse platea dictumst. Suspendisse posuere vehicula
libero in varius. Suspendisse potenti. Mauris sit amet odio in
felis varius accumsan. In vitae sem ipsum. Fusce faucibus sem id
ligula ornare posuere vehicula elit porta. Ut ac est felis. Sed et
imperdiet nisl. Donec nec imperdiet enim. Sed metus nisl, rutrum in
interdum at, elementum eu elit. Vivamus non sapien nec dui
vestibulum suscipit nec vel metus. Suspendisse potenti. Proin
pellentesque, dui eget congue elementum, ante purus pharetra metus,
eget bibendum lacus neque lacinia est. Morbi rutrum diam sit amet
tellus faucibus egestas. Sed quam lectus, adipiscing eget placerat
in, laoreet eget ipsum.<p>

<p>Vestibulum viverra, velit non molestie ultrices, dolor nibh
vulputate erat, quis luctus ligula sem eu lacus. Nunc ullamcorper,
nibh in iaculis gravida, arcu justo luctus neque, ut laoreet erat
lorem vitae erat. Sed dapibus ligula tempus augue ultricies dictum.
Morbi scelerisque nisi fringilla sem ultricies imperdiet. Lorem
ipsum dolor sit amet, consectetur adipiscing elit. Class aptent
taciti sociosqu ad litora torquent per conubia nostra, per inceptos
himenaeos. Nunc sagittis vestibulum est, non pulvinar tellus
convallis nec. Duis sit amet ligula eu ante vehicula laoreet id sed
odio. Aliquam erat volutpat. Proin nisl augue, hendrerit in porta
in, mattis egestas orci. Cras vel aliquet quam. Aenean gravida,
odio et ullamcorper tincidunt, neque est fringilla mi, vel commodo
risus augue non felis.</p>
    </div>
    <a href="#top">Top</a>
</body>
</html>

This is how the styling will look when viewed in the browser. Both **visited and unvisited links appear the same**.

This is how **hover style** appears when the user is hovering over the link. Notice that the "Putting in the Time" **link is now underlined**.

Questions for Review

1. Which selector can be used to change the color of the link?
a. a:website
b. a:class
c. a:anchor
d. a:link

2. If you want to make the link color change to blue after the user has clicked the link, what pseudo-class attribute would you use?
a. a:visited {color:blue; }
b. a: color=blue;
c. a:color:red
d. a: visited:red

3. How would you change the text of a link to bold?

a. a:link{ text-weight: b }
b. a:link{ text-weight:bold; }
c. a:link{ font-weight:bold; }
d. a:link{ font-weight:b }

4. If you want a link underlined when a user hovers over it, which would be the correct pseudo-class selector syntax?
a. a:click{ text-decoration: strikethrough;
b. a:hover{ text-decoration: underline;
c. a:hover{ text-decoration:strikethrough
d. a:click{ text-decoration: underline;

Chapter 4 Lab Exercises

1) Create a correct and standard-compliant HTML 4.01 basic document structure. Inside the **<title>** element, place the text **Lab 4: Links**.

2) Place an **<h1>** element at the top of the page, just underneath the opening <body> tag. Place the text "**My Favorite Sites**" in the <h1> element.

3) Place the following text after the <h1> element. You may line break by using either **<p>** elements or **
** tags.

For news I watch CNN.
I get my tech news from TWiT.
I am learning HTML with LearnToProgram.tv.
I purchase a lot of gear from Amazon.
Everyone should donate money to the American Cancer Society.

4) Create links to the following addresses. Be careful to select the text indicated as the link text—the part of the text that the user can click to activate the link.

Link Text	Link
CNN	http://www.cnn.com
TWiT	http://www.twit.tv
Learning HTML	http://www.learntoprogram.tv
Amazon	http://www.amazon.com
American Cancer Society	http://www.cancer.org

5) Create a **<style>** element with appropriate attributes in the **<head>** section of the document.

6) Using the CSS styling, adjust the appearance of the links so that they always appear dark gray. They become underlined only when the user hovers their mouse over the link text.

7) Below the link "American Cancer Society", add text that says "See my other page…" Place this text as a **<p>** element.

8) Create a new HTML page using the correct document structure for HTML 4.01. In the page, place the text "This is my other page. Go back to my first page" in the document **<body>** using **<p>** tags.

9) Use "Go back to my first page" as link text to create a link back to the first page you created.

10) On the original page you created, create a link to the new page you created using "See my other page…" as link text.

11) Load the file lab_starter.html, which is provided with the course in your text editor. The link texts found at the top of the page correspond to the <h3> headings throughout the document.

12) Created named anchors on all of the <h3> tags. Link those named anchors in the document page. Your links should appear in the section of the code that looks like this:

```
<h2>Featuring Anchors</h2>
<p>In the Beginning</br>
This is my Story<br/>
Two Cats and a Cheap Couch<br/>
Finding Myself<br/>
How it Ended</p>
```

13) Create an anchor and link pair that allows the user to move from the "Back to Top" text at the bottom of the page to the very top of the page.

14) Apply the CSS you created in step 6 to this document so that links appear dark gray and are only underlined when the user is hovering above them.

Lab Solution – Main Page (1-7)

```
<!DOCTYPE HTML PUBLIC "-//W3C//DTD HTML 4.01//EN"
    "http://www.w3.org/TR/html4/strict.dtd"
    >
<html lang="en">
<head>
    <title>Lab 4: Links</title>
    <style type="text/css">
    h2  {
            font-family: Georgia, serif;
            font-size: 1.75em;

    }
    p   {
            font-family: Helvetica, Arial, sans-serif;
            font-size: .8em;

    }
    a:link, a:visited{
            color: gray;
            font-weight: bold;
            text-decoration: none;

    }
    a:hover{
            color: gray;
            font-weight: bold;
            text-decoration: underline;

    }

    </style>
</head>
<body>
    <h1>My Favorite Sites</h1>
    <p>For news I watch <a href="http://www.cnn.com">CNN.</a></p>
    <p>I get my tech news from <a
href="http://www.twit.com">TWiT.</a></p>
    <p>I am learning HTML with <a
href="http://www.learntoprogram.tv">LearnToProgram.tv.</a></p>
    <p>I purchase a lot of gear from <a
href="http://www.amazon.com">Amazon.</a></p>
    <p>Everyone should donate money to the <a
href="http://www.cancer.org">American Cancer Society.</a></p>
```

```
    <p>See my <a href="otherpage.html">other page</a></p>

</body>
</html>
```

Lab Solution – Lab Starter (8-10)

```
<!DOCTYPE HTML PUBLIC "-//W3C//DTD HTML 4.01//EN"
    "http://www.w3.org/TR/html4/strict.dtd"
    >
<html lang="en">
<head>
    <title>This is my other page</title>
<style type="text/css">
    h2  {
            font-family: Georgia, serif;
            font-size: 1.75em;

    }
    p   {

            font-family: Helvetica, Arial, sans-serif;
            font-size: .8em;

    }
        a:link, a:visited{
            color: gray;
            font-weight: bold;
            text-decoration: none;

    }
        a:hover{
            color: gray;
            font-weight: bold;
            text-decoration: underline;

    }

    </style>

</head>
<body>
    <p>This is my other page</p>
     <p>Go <a href="lab4links.html">back</a> to my main page</p>
</body>
</html>
```

Lab Solution – Other Page (11-14)

```html
<!DOCTYPE HTML PUBLIC "-//W3C//DTD HTML 4.01//EN"
    "http://www.w3.org/TR/html4/strict.dtd"
    >
<html lang="en">
<head>
    <title>Anchor Lab Exercise</title>
    <style type="text/css">
    h2  {
            font-family: Georgia, serif;
            font-size: 1.75em;

    }
    p   {
            font-family: Helvetica, Arial, sans-serif;
            font-size: .8em;

    }
        a:link, a:visited{
            color: gray;
            font-weight: bold;
            text-decoration: none;
    }
        a:hover{
            color: gray;
            font-weight: bold;
            text-decoration: underline;

    }

    </style>
</head>

<body>
    <h1>A Page Full of Gibberish</h1>
    <h2>Featuring Anchors</h2>
    <a name="top"/>
    <a href="#beginning">In the Beginning</a></br>
    <a href="#story">This is my Story</a><br/>
    <a href="#cats">Two Cats and a Cheap Couch</a><br/>
    <a href="#finding">Finding Myself</a><br/>
    <a href="#ended">How it Ended</a></p>

    <h3><a name="beginning"/>In the Beginning</h3>
  <p>Lorem ipsum dolor sit amet, consectetur adipiscing elit.
Aliquam sollicitudin ligula a nisl tempus laoreet. Donec et leo in
felis sagittis placerat et at massa. Cras suscipit iaculis dolor, a
ultrices arcu facilisis vitae. Aliquam ac felis vel est rhoncus
congue aliquam ut augue. Pellentesque tincidunt enim libero.
Integer turpis sapien, vehicula a lacinia vitae, eleifend sit amet
metus. Praesent hendrerit auctor dui quis sodales. Vestibulum
placerat sem vitae lorem mollis nec laoreet metus luctus. Nulla
laoreet erat interdum mauris congue quis suscipit mi aliquet. Nulla
auctor ultrices ipsum, mattis molestie tellus varius a. Vivamus
eget dapibus est. Integer vitae leo pellentesque tellus venenatis
elementum sed ut diam. Sed vel feugiat dolor. Morbi vel nulla sed
felis auctor cursus. Proin turpis velit, mattis eu vulputate sit
amet, eleifend a dui. Aenean non blandit sapien.</p>

    <p>Nunc ac ipsum quis nisi ullamcorper aliquet. Fusce nisi
dolor, sollicitudin ac sollicitudin sed, gravida sed turpis. Ut id
```

velit vitae urna ornare pharetra. Morbi nunc velit, consectetur vel
pulvinar et, tempor sit amet magna. Class aptent taciti sociosqu ad
litora torquent per conubia nostra, per inceptos himenaeos. Sed id
leo velit. Nam vel nibh ut est iaculis elementum. Fusce malesuada
velit sit amet nulla faucibus in blandit arcu ultricies. In auctor,
metus id vehicula tincidunt, magna lectus sollicitudin ipsum, quis
porttitor felis elit vehicula sem. Donec ultricies neque sit amet
elit pellentesque laoreet. Mauris id augue faucibus urna porta
porta ut ac enim. Quisque ultrices bibendum metus ornare
ullamcorper. Nulla sapien nibh, scelerisque ac convallis ac,
consectetur id lacus. Etiam vitae augue vitae tortor tincidunt
porta et quis tellus. Cras nunc lorem, aliquam non tempor vel,
pharetra vel purus.</p>
    <p>Duis sed tempor arcu. Ut tortor urna, ultrices nec auctor
non, interdum suscipit dolor. Phasellus condimentum leo a metus
adipiscing euismod. Sed adipiscing neque elementum quam ultricies
aliquam. Integer sodales, dolor nec sagittis placerat, risus lectus
pretium enim, et consectetur sem odio sit amet massa. Mauris velit
felis, congue ut varius ut, commodo vel nulla. Nulla nec suscipit
leo.</p>
    <h3><a name="story"/>This is my Story</h3>
    <p>Lorem ipsum dolor sit amet, consectetur adipiscing elit.
Aliquam sollicitudin ligula a nisl tempus laoreet. Donec et leo in
felis sagittis placerat et at massa. Cras suscipit iaculis dolor, a
ultrices arcu facilisis vitae. Aliquam ac felis vel est rhoncus
congue aliquam ut augue. Pellentesque tincidunt enim libero.
Integer turpis sapien, vehicula a lacinia vitae, eleifend sit amet
metus. Praesent hendrerit auctor dui quis sodales. Vestibulum
placerat sem vitae lorem mollis nec laoreet metus luctus. Nulla
laoreet erat interdum mauris congue quis suscipit mi aliquet. Nulla
auctor ultrices ipsum, mattis molestie tellus varius a. Vivamus
eget dapibus est. Integer vitae leo pellentesque tellus venenatis
elementum sed ut diam. Sed vel feugiat dolor. Morbi vel nulla sed
felis auctor cursus. Proin turpis velit, mattis eu vulputate sit
amet, eleifend a dui. Aenean non blandit sapien.</p>
    <p>Nunc ac ipsum quis nisi ullamcorper aliquet. Fusce nisi
dolor, sollicitudin ac sollicitudin sed, gravida sed turpis. Ut id
velit vitae urna ornare pharetra. Morbi nunc velit, consectetur vel
pulvinar et, tempor sit amet magna. Class aptent taciti sociosqu ad
litora torquent per conubia nostra, per inceptos himenaeos. Sed id
leo velit. Nam vel nibh ut est iaculis elementum. Fusce malesuada
velit sit amet nulla faucibus in blandit arcu ultricies. In auctor,
metus id vehicula tincidunt, magna lectus sollicitudin ipsum, quis
porttitor felis elit vehicula sem. Donec ultricies neque sit amet
elit pellentesque laoreet. Mauris id augue faucibus urna porta
porta ut ac enim. Quisque ultrices bibendum metus ornare
ullamcorper. Nulla sapien nibh, scelerisque ac convallis ac,
consectetur id lacus. Etiam vitae augue vitae tortor tincidunt
porta et quis tellus. Cras nunc lorem, aliquam non tempor vel,
pharetra vel purus.</p>
    <p>Duis sed tempor arcu. Ut tortor urna, ultrices nec auctor
non, interdum suscipit dolor. Phasellus condimentum leo a metus
adipiscing euismod. Sed adipiscing neque elementum quam ultricies
aliquam. Integer sodales, dolor nec sagittis placerat, risus lectus
pretium enim, et consectetur sem odio sit amet massa. Mauris velit
felis, congue ut varius ut, commodo vel nulla. Nulla nec suscipit
leo.</p>
    <h3><a name="cats"/>Two Cats and a Cheap Couch</h3>
    <p>Lorem ipsum dolor sit amet, consectetur adipiscing elit.
Aliquam sollicitudin ligula a nisl tempus laoreet. Donec et leo in

felis sagittis placerat et at massa. Cras suscipit iaculis dolor, a
ultrices arcu facilisis vitae. Aliquam ac felis vel est rhoncus
congue aliquam ut augue. Pellentesque tincidunt enim libero.
Integer turpis sapien, vehicula a lacinia vitae, eleifend sit amet
metus. Praesent hendrerit auctor dui quis sodales. Vestibulum
placerat sem vitae lorem mollis nec laoreet metus luctus. Nulla
laoreet erat interdum mauris congue quis suscipit mi aliquet. Nulla
auctor ultrices ipsum, mattis molestie tellus varius a. Vivamus
eget dapibus est. Integer vitae leo pellentesque tellus venenatis
elementum sed ut diam. Sed vel feugiat dolor. Morbi vel nulla sed
felis auctor cursus. Proin turpis velit, mattis eu vulputate sit
amet, eleifend a dui. Aenean non blandit sapien.</p>
    <p>Nunc ac ipsum quis nisi ullamcorper aliquet. Fusce nisi
dolor, sollicitudin ac sollicitudin sed, gravida sed turpis. Ut id
velit vitae urna ornare pharetra. Morbi nunc velit, consectetur vel
pulvinar et, tempor sit amet magna. Class aptent taciti sociosqu ad
litora torquent per conubia nostra, per inceptos himenaeos. Sed id
leo velit. Nam vel nibh ut est iaculis elementum. Fusce malesuada
velit sit amet nulla faucibus in blandit arcu ultricies. In auctor,
metus id vehicula tincidunt, magna lectus sollicitudin ipsum, quis
porttitor felis elit vehicula sem. Donec ultricies neque sit amet
elit pellentesque laoreet. Mauris id augue faucibus urna porta
porta ut ac enim. Quisque ultrices bibendum metus ornare
ullamcorper. Nulla sapien nibh, scelerisque ac convallis ac,
consectetur id lacus. Etiam vitae augue vitae tortor tincidunt
porta et quis tellus. Cras nunc lorem, aliquam non tempor vel,
pharetra vel purus.</p>
    <p>Duis sed tempor arcu. Ut tortor urna, ultrices nec auctor
non, interdum suscipit dolor. Phasellus condimentum leo a metus
adipiscing euismod. Sed adipiscing neque elementum quam ultricies
aliquam. Integer sodales, dolor nec sagittis placerat, risus lectus
pretium enim, et consectetur sem odio sit amet massa. Mauris velit
felis, congue ut varius ut, commodo vel nulla. Nulla nec suscipit
leo.</p>
    <h3><a name="finding"/>Finding Myself</h3>
    <p>Lorem ipsum dolor sit amet, consectetur adipiscing elit.
Aliquam sollicitudin ligula a nisl tempus laoreet. Donec et leo in
felis sagittis placerat et at massa. Cras suscipit iaculis dolor, a
ultrices arcu facilisis vitae. Aliquam ac felis vel est rhoncus
congue aliquam ut augue. Pellentesque tincidunt enim libero.
Integer turpis sapien, vehicula a lacinia vitae, eleifend sit amet
metus. Praesent hendrerit auctor dui quis sodales. Vestibulum
placerat sem vitae lorem mollis nec laoreet metus luctus. Nulla
laoreet erat interdum mauris congue quis suscipit mi aliquet. Nulla
auctor ultrices ipsum, mattis molestie tellus varius a. Vivamus
eget dapibus est. Integer vitae leo pellentesque tellus venenatis
elementum sed ut diam. Sed vel feugiat dolor. Morbi vel nulla sed
felis auctor cursus. Proin turpis velit, mattis eu vulputate sit
amet, eleifend a dui. Aenean non blandit sapien.</p>
    <p>Nunc ac ipsum quis nisi ullamcorper aliquet. Fusce nisi
dolor, sollicitudin ac sollicitudin sed, gravida sed turpis. Ut id
velit vitae urna ornare pharetra. Morbi nunc velit, consectetur vel
pulvinar et, tempor sit amet magna. Class aptent taciti sociosqu ad
litora torquent per conubia nostra, per inceptos himenaeos. Sed id
leo velit. Nam vel nibh ut est iaculis elementum. Fusce malesuada
velit sit amet nulla faucibus in blandit arcu ultricies. In auctor,
metus id vehicula tincidunt, magna lectus sollicitudin ipsum, quis
porttitor felis elit vehicula sem. Donec ultricies neque sit amet
elit pellentesque laoreet. Mauris id augue faucibus urna porta
porta ut ac enim. Quisque ultrices bibendum metus ornare

ullamcorper. Nulla sapien nibh, scelerisque ac convallis ac, consectetur id lacus. Etiam vitae augue vitae tortor tincidunt porta et quis tellus. Cras nunc lorem, aliquam non tempor vel, pharetra vel purus.</p>
<p>Duis sed tempor arcu. Ut tortor urna, ultrices nec auctor non, interdum suscipit dolor. Phasellus condimentum leo a metus adipiscing euismod. Sed adipiscing neque elementum quam ultricies aliquam. Integer sodales, dolor nec sagittis placerat, risus lectus pretium enim, et consectetur sem odio sit amet massa. Mauris velit felis, congue ut varius ut, commodo vel nulla. Nulla nec suscipit leo.</p>
<h3><a name="ended"/>How it Ended</h3>

<p>Nunc ac ipsum quis nisi ullamcorper aliquet. Fusce nisi dolor, sollicitudin ac sollicitudin sed, gravida sed turpis. Ut id velit vitae urna ornare pharetra. Morbi nunc velit, consectetur vel pulvinar et, tempor sit amet magna. Class aptent taciti sociosqu ad litora torquent per conubia nostra, per inceptos himenaeos. Sed id leo velit. Nam vel nibh ut est iaculis elementum. Fusce malesuada velit sit amet nulla faucibus in blandit arcu ultricies. In auctor, metus id vehicula tincidunt, magna lectus sollicitudin ipsum, quis porttitor felis elit vehicula sem. Donec ultricies neque sit amet elit pellentesque laoreet. Mauris id augue faucibus urna porta porta ut ac enim. Quisque ultrices bibendum metus ornare ullamcorper. Nulla sapien nibh, scelerisque ac convallis ac, consectetur id lacus. Etiam vitae augue vitae tortor tincidunt porta et quis tellus. Cras nunc lorem, aliquam non tempor vel, pharetra vel purus.</p>
<p>Duis sed tempor arcu. Ut tortor urna, ultrices nec auctor non, interdum suscipit dolor. Phasellus condimentum leo a metus adipiscing euismod. Sed adipiscing neque elementum quam ultricies aliquam. Integer sodales, dolor nec sagittis placerat, risus lectus pretium enim, et consectetur sem odio sit amet massa. Mauris velit felis, congue ut varius ut, commodo vel nulla. Nulla nec suscipit leo.</p>
<a href="#top"><strong>Back to Top,</strong></a>
</body>
</html>

Chapter 4 Summary

In this chapter, we discussed how to create internal and external links on a webpage and how to use anchor links to easily navigate within a page.

You also learned how to use CSS pseudo-class styling—changing the link color before and after it is visited and when the user hovers over it with a mouse.

The next chapter discusses displaying pictures in your website, and audio and video embedding using HTML5.

Chapter 5: Working with Images and Media

Chapter Objectives:
•Students will be able to insert images into their webpages.
•Students will be able to format the text to flow around pictures.
•Students will be able to embed audio into their webpages using HTML5.
• Students will be able to place video on their webpages using HTML5.

5.1 Displaying Images, Image Links and Image Styling with CSS

This chapter will discuss how to display images using HTML.

Displaying images in an HTML page is easy. Elements used are **<img>** tag and the **src** attribute. As an example, using one of the image files above, javascript.png, the image source tag would be:

```
<img src="javascript.png"/>
```

When inserting your image, it is recommended that you include the attribute for alternative text—**alt**. It provides a text representation for the image when the user is browsing without the image turned on or when your mobile device has a slow connection. To use the alt attribute, write it after the file name. If we add the alternative text for the above example, the code will be as follows:

```
<img src="javascript.png" alt="Mark Lassoff's Javascript Course"/>
```

When the image cannot be displayed, the browser will default to displaying the text "Mark Lassoff's Javascript Course".

There are times you want an image to function like a link. It is possible to make an image work just like a text link. To do that, use the anchor tag **<a>** with the **href** attribute. Let us use the image **logo_200.png** with the alternative text "LearnTo Program.tv logo". To insert the image and create its link, start your code with an anchor tag with href attribute followed by the image tag and source value, then finally the alternative text. The code should be as follows:

```
<a href="http://www.learntoprogram.tv"><img src="logo_200.png"
alt="LearnToProgram.tv logo"/></a>
```

Some browsers by default put a border around images. When borders are not preferred, CSS styling can be used to prevent it from being displayed. This is done by setting the border **attribute** of the **image selector to 0px**, thus removing the unwanted border. The CSS code should now be:

```
<style type="text/css">
    img   {
  border: 0px;
          }
</style>
```

One of the important things to consider in HTML is how the images interact with the text on the website. In this example, we have pasted some text into our document to see how it interacts with the image.

By default and without any style change, the image simply sits on the same line and texts do not flow around the image. However, in some instances, you would want the text to flow around the image. To do this, include in the image tag **align=** attribute whose value can be set to right or left. This will allow the text to flow around the image. Using the previous image tag and after including the align attribute, the code will now be as follows:

```
<a href=http://www.learntoprogram.tv><img src="logo_200.png"
alt="LearnToProgram.tv logo" align=right/></a>
```

A more convenient way to design the look of your web page is by using CSS, which will be introduced later in the course. Below is the complete code listing of an example including an image.

Code Listing: Displaying Images

```
<!DOCTYPE HTML PUBLIC "-//W3C//DTD HTML 4.01//EN"
    "http://www.w3.org/TR/html4/strict.dtd"
    >
<html lang="en">
<head>
    <title>Displaying Images</title>
    <style type="text/css">
        img {
            border: 0px;
        }
    </style>
</head>
<body>
    <img src="javascript.png" alt="Mark Lassoff's Javascript
Course"/>
    <br/>
    <p><a href="http://www.learntoprogram.tv"><img
src="logo_200.png" alt="LearnToProgram.tv logo" align="right"
/></a>
    Lorem ipsum dolor sit amet, consectetur adipiscing elit.
Vestibulum luctus interdum dui, nec euismod tellus volutpat nec.
Phasellus malesuada venenatis sapien, et accumsan odio congue eu.
Etiam faucibus vulputate tellus, sed semper dui euismod vitae.
Vivamus nisi tellus, ullamcorper eget semper non, viverra quis
erat. Mauris blandit placerat elit a bibendum. Integer at urna
vitae risus bibendum iaculis. Nullam ullamcorper, risus facilisis
tempor congue, tortor magna sollicitudin nulla, at tempor diam
lectus sed erat. Nam fermentum mi sit amet diam tincidunt eget
eleifend arcu facilisis.
    </p>
</body>
</html>
```

This is what the webpage will look like when viewed in the browser:

Questions for Review

1. What tag should you use to display "imagefile.png" on a webpage?
a. <img src="imagefile.png"/>
b. img src=imagefile.png
c. <pic src="imagefile.png">
d. pic src=imagefile.png

2. What is the purpose of placing an alt attribute in your image tag?
a. To place an alternative image for users of different web browsers.
b. To place an alternative image for users from different operating systems.
c. To place text in place of the picture for users who have image viewing turned off.
d. To redirect a user to a different website.

3. What CSS attribute should you add to your webpage to make sure you don't have any borders around a picture with a link?
a. img { border=none;}
b. img { border=0px; }
c. img { border=0;}
d. img { border=null;}

4. What attribute tag should you use to get the text to flow around your image?
a. flow=
b. Layout=
c. Place=
d. align=

5.2 HTML5 Audio Embeds

In this section we are going to discuss the audio capabilities of HTML5. In previous versions of HTML, users need a plugin for audio and video, such as QuickTime, RealPlayer or Flash. The problem was, not everyone had the same plugins and a website could alienate its audience by using a specific plugin. HTML5 solves this problem with the audio tag.

When using the audio tag it is a good idea to include multiple file formats to make sure a user's browser supports the audio. Not all browsers support every file type, so the audio tag allows you to include as many formats as you want.

In this example we will use the files **mark.aif, mark.wav** and **mark.mp3** so that there is at least one audio file that will be played by the browser.

To cue insertion of the audio file, the audio tag **<audio>** will be used in conjunction with **controls** so the user can start or stop the audio. The tag is as follows:

```
<audio controls="controls">
```

In order to link to the actual music file, the source tag file must be given the audio file name and the audio file type. The source tag for an mp3 file is:

```
<source src="mark.mp3" type="audio/mp3"/>
```

In case the browser doesn't support any of the file types, it will be a good idea to include a message telling the user that the browser doesn't support the audio file. Here is the code that demonstrates audio file insertion in your webpage. Ensure that HTML5 is the document type used in order to play the audio in the browser.

Code Listing: HTML5 Audio Embeds

```
<!DOCTYPE html>

<html>
<head>
    <title>Audio</title>
</head>

<body>
    <audio controls="controls">
        <source src="mark.mp3" type="audio/mp3"/>
        <source src="mark.wav" type="audio/wav"/>
        <source src="mark.aif" type="audio/aif"/>
        Your Browser doesn't support the audio file format
available.
    </audio>
</body>
</html>
```

Questions for Review

1. What audio embedding change does HTML5 introduce when compared with previous versions?
a. It's more stylish.
b. It plays more loudly.
c. It plays more slowly.
d. It no longer requires a third party plugin.

2. What attribute value do you use in your HTML to give the user control over the audio?
a. <audio controls="controls">
b. <audio play="play">
c. <audio go="go">
d. <audio button="button">

3. What is the correct source tag if you want to embed an audio file named play.wav?
a. <source src="play.wav" type="audio/mp3"/>
b. <source src="play.wav" type="audio/aif"/>
c. <source src="play.wav" type="audio/wav"/>
d. <src="play.wav" type="audio/mp3"/>

4. Why is it important to supply several different formats of audio in HTML5?
a. A user might prefer a certain format.
b. To ensure that whichever browser is used, it will find a format it supports and play the audio.
c. Because audio format download differs by computer.
d. Users find it exciting.

5.3 HTML5 Video Embeds

In this section we are going to examine how to play a video file with HTML5. The process is very similar to embedding audio. What would differ, of course, is the tag used, **<video>,** but it includes the same control. The HTML5 video tag is as follows:

```
<video controls="controls">
```

Let us use the video file QualitySample.mp4 in our example. To cue insertion of the video file, the video tag <video> will be used in conjunction with **controls** so the user can start or stop the audio. The tag is as follows:

```
<source src="QualitySample.mp4" type="video/mp4" />
```

However, you may sometimes need to change the size of the video to accommodate the browser. It's important to note that when the size of the video is changed, you need to make sure the aspect ratio of the video is maintained so it does not get distorted. In order to change the size in the video tag, add the width and height attributes.

Code Listing: HTML5 Video Embeds

```
<!DOCTYPE html>

<html>
<head>
    <title>Page Title</title>
</head>

<body>

<video controls="controls" width="640" height="360">
    <source src="QualitySample.mp4" type="video/mp4" />
    Your Browser does not support the video format available.
</video>
</body>
</html>
```

This is how the video will look when viewed in the browser. Keep in mind that it will look different in every browser and some may not support the mp4 format.

Questions for Review

1. What tag is used in embedding video in HTML5?
a. <audio controls="controls">
b. <video controls="controls">
c. <video controls="controls" width="640" height="360">
d. <video control="embed">

2. What attribute do you use to set the size and width of a video file?
a. <video controls="controls" width=" " height=" ">
b. <source src="video file name.type" type="video/type" />
c. Video=<width= height=
d. <audio controls="controls"width="" height="">

3. How do you specify the video file source and its type when embedding video in HTML5?
a. <video src="video file name.type" type="video/type" />
b. Browsers will change the size of video formats.
c. <source src="video file name.type" type="video/type" />
d. <source=video, type>

Chapter 5 Lab Exercises

1) Create a correct and standard-compliant HTML 4.01 basic document structure. Inside the <title> element, place the text **Lab 5: Images**. Save the page as **page1.html**.

2) Download and decompress the sample images .zip that comes with the course. Change the name of the folder to **images**. Place that folder inside the folder that holds your HTML file.

3) On the page you are editing, using correct HTML code, place the image called **bank.png** on the page. Using CSS, remove any border that might appear around the image in certain browsers.

4) Below the image **add the caption** "This is the former home of Westport Bank and Trust. It is now a Patagonia retail store. This building was constructed in the 1800s."

5) **Style the caption** so it has the following properties:

Font: Arial
Font Size: .75em
Color: Dark Blue

6) Below the caption, **place the text Next and Previous**. Style the text so it matches the caption, but **is a different color**.

7) Create three more HTML pages. Use a naming convention that makes sense to you for the page file names. For example, you could name the pages page2.html, page3.html, and page4.html.

8) Place contents on each page accordingly:

Page	Image	Caption
Page 2	River.png	The Saugatuck River runs through Westport and provides a favorite fishing spot for many locals.
Page 3	Tavern.png	The Tavern on Main in Westport's downtown has been a favorite watering hole for locals for years.
Page 4	townHall.png	Westport's historic Town Hall is not just the seat of local government, but also has an impressive display of art and an auditorium used for town functions.

9) Add the next and previous text to each of the pages you just created.

10) Go through all four pages and add code so that the next and previous text become links to the previous and next pages. If the user clicks next on page 1 they should move to page 2. If the user clicks next on page 4 they should return to page 1, and so on.

11) Make your CSS external and use the <link> tag with correct attributes on all pages to link to the CSS. This will give all of your pages a consistent look.

12) Test to ensure that there are no broken links and that all pages appear consistently styled.

Lab Solution – Page1.html

```
<!DOCTYPE HTML PUBLIC "-//W3C//DTD HTML 4.01//EN"
    "http://www.w3.org/TR/html4/strict.dtd"
    >
<head>
    <title>Displaying Images</title>
    <style type="text/css">
        img {
                border: 0px;
            }
        p   {

                color: #000080;
                font-family: arial;
                font-size: .75em;
            }
    </style>
</head>
<body>
    <img src="/images/bank.png" alt="Patagonia Retail Store" /><br>
    <p>This is the former home of Westport Bank and Trust.  It is
now a Patagonia retail store.  This building was constructed in the
1800s.</p>
    <p> <font color=green>Next and Previous</font></p>
</body>
</html>
```

Replace bold text with your file's pathname.

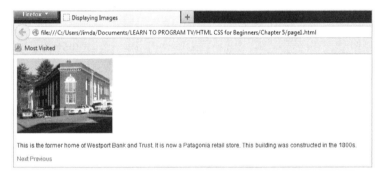

page2.html

```
<!DOCTYPE HTML PUBLIC "-//W3C//DTD HTML 4.01//EN"
    "http://www.w3.org/TR/html4/strict.dtd"
    >
<head>
    <title>Displaying Images</title>

</head>
<body>
<style type="text/css">
        img    {
                        border: 0px;
               }
        p      {

                        color: #000080;
                        font-family: arial;
                        font-size: .75em;
               }
    </style>

    <img src="/images/river.png" alt="The Saugatuck River" /><br>
    <p>The Saugatuck River runs through Westport and provides a
favorite fishing spot for many locals.</p>
    <p> <font color=green>Next Previous</font></p>
</body>
</html>
```

Replace bold text with your file's pathname. page2.html will contain details for The Saugatuck River with the image river.png.

page3.html

```
<!DOCTYPE HTML PUBLIC "-//W3C//DTD HTML 4.01//EN"
    "http://www.w3.org/TR/html4/strict.dtd"
>
<head>
    <title>Displaying Images</title>

</head>
<body>
<style type="text/css">
        img     {
                        border: 0px;
                }
        p       {
                        color: #000080;
                        font-family: arial;
                        font-size: .75em;
                }
    </style>

    <img src="/images/tavern.png" alt="The Tavern" /><br>
    <p>The Tavern on Main in Westport's downtown has been a
favorite watering hole for locals for years.</p>
    <p> <font color=green>Next Previous</font></p>
</body>
</html>
```

Replace bold text with your file's pathname. page3.html will contain details for The Tavern with the image tavern.png.

page4.html

```
<!DOCTYPE HTML PUBLIC "-//W3C//DTD HTML 4.01//EN"
    "http://www.w3.org/TR/html4/strict.dtd"
    >
<head>
    <title>Displaying Images</title>

</head>
<body>
<style type="text/css">
        img     {
                        border: 0px;
                }
        p       {
                        color: #000080;
                        font-family: arial;
                        font-size: .75em;
                }
    </style>

    <img src="/images/townHall.png" alt="The Town Hall" /><br>
    <p>Westport's historic town is not just the seat of local
government, but also has an impressive display of art and an
auditorium used for town functions.</p>
    <p> <font color=green>Next Previous </font></p>
</body>
</html>
```

Replace bold text with your file's pathname. page4.html will contain details for The Tavern with the image tavern.png.

130

Lab Solution I – Image embedding, external CSS
page1excss.html

```
<!DOCTYPE HTML PUBLIC "-//W3C//DTD HTML 4.01//EN"
    "http://www.w3.org/TR/html4/strict.dtd"
>
<html>
<head>
    <title>Displaying Images</title>
    <style  type="text/css" href="ch5labexSol.css">
    </style>
</head>

<body>

    <img src="/images/bank.png" alt="Patagonia Retail Store" /><br>
    <p>This is the former home of Westport Bank and Trust.  It is
now a Patagonia retail store.  This building was constructed in the
1800s.</p>
    <p>
        <a href="page4excss.html">Previous</a>
        <a href="page2excss.html">Next</a></p>
</body>
</html>
```

Create another html page so as not to disrupt the previous outputs.
page1excss.html contains the Patagonia retail store details and styling is in the file
named ch5labexSol.css. Replace bold text with your file's pathname.

page2excss.html

```
<!DOCTYPE HTML PUBLIC "-//W3C//DTD HTML 4.01//EN"
    "http://www.w3.org/TR/html4/strict.dtd"
    >
<head>
    <title>Displaying Images</title>
    <style type="text/css" href="ch5LabSol.css"></style>
</head>
<body>
    <img src="/images/river.png" alt="The Saugatuck River" /><br>
    <p>The Saugatuck River runs through Westport and provides a
favorite fishing spot for many locals.</p>
    <p>
        <a href="page1excss.html">Previous</a>
        <a href="page3excss.html">Next</a></p>
<body>
</html>
```

Create another html page so as not to disrupt the previous outputs.
page2excss.html contains the Saugatuck River details, while styling is in the file
named ch5LabSol.css. Replace bold text with your file's pathname.

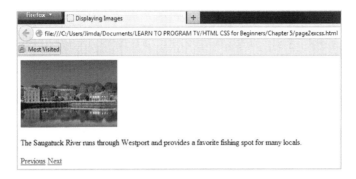

The Saugatuck River runs through Westport and provides a favorite fishing spot for many locals.

Previous Next

page3excss.html

```
<!DOCTYPE HTML PUBLIC "-//W3C//DTD HTML 4.01//EN"
    "http://www.w3.org/TR/html4/strict.dtd"
>
<head>
    <title>Displaying Images</title>
    <style type="text/css" href="ch5LabSol.css"></style>
</head>
<body>
    <img src="/images/tavern.png" alt="The Tavern"  /><br>
    <p>The Tavern on Main in Westport's downtown has been a
favorite watering hole for locals for years.</p>
    <p>
        <a href="page2excss.html">Previous</a>
        <a href="page4excss.html">Next</a></p>
</body>
</html>
```

Create another html page named **page3excss.html** which will contain the Tavern's details, while styling is in the file named ch5LabSol.css. Replace bold text with your file's pathname.

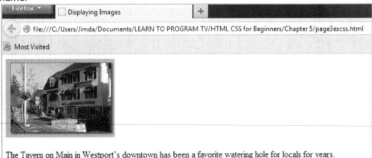

The Tavern on Main in Westport's downtown has been a favorite watering hole for locals for years.

Previous Next

page4excss.html

```
<!DOCTYPE HTML PUBLIC "-//W3C//DTD HTML 4.01//EN"
    "http://www.w3.org/TR/html4/strict.dtd"
    >
<head>
```

```
        <title>Displaying Images</title>
        <style type="text/css" href="ch5LabSol.css"></style>
</head>
<body>
        <img src="/images/townHall.png" alt="The Town Hall"  /><br>
        <p>Westport's historic Town Hall is not just the seat of local
government, but also has an impressive display of art and
auditorium used for town functions.</p>
        <p>
            <a href="page3excss.html">Previous</a>
            <a href="page1excss.html">Next</a></p>
</body>
</html>
```

Create another html page named **page4excss.html** which will contain the Tavern's
details, while styling is in the file named ch5LabSol.css. Replace bold text with your file's
pathname.

Lab Solution I – External CSS filename: ch5LabSol.css

```
img     {
            border: 0px;
        }
p       {
            color: #000080;
            font-family: arial, verdana, sans-serif;
            font-size:.75em;
        }
a:link  {
            color:green;
            text-decoration: none;
        }
```

Lab Solution II -- Audio and Video embedding

```
<?xml version="1.0" encoding="UTF-8"?>
<!DOCTYPE html PUBLIC "-//W3C//DTD XHTML 1.0 Strict//EN"
"http://www.w3.org/TR/xhtml1/DTD/xhtml1-strict.dtd">
<html xmlns="http://www.w3.org/1999/xhtml" xml:lang="en" lang="en">
<head>
    <title>My Audio</title>
</head>
<body>
    <h1>My Audio</h1>
    <audio controls="controls">
        <source src="mark.mp3" type="audio/mp3"/>
        <source src="mark.wav" type="audio/wav"/>
        <source src="mark.aif" type="audio/aif"/>
        Your Browser doesn't support the audio file format
available.
    </audio>

    <h1>My Video</h1>
    <video controls="controls" width="640" height="360">
        <source src="movie.mp4" type="video/mp4"/>
Your Browser doesn't support the audio file format available.
</video>
</body>
</html>
```

Browser's output/display.

Chapter 5 Summary

In this chapter we discussed how to place images onto a website and how to format the text around the image in order to create a more pleasing look to the webpage.

You also learned how to embed audio and video using HTML5. We reviewed the importance of using multiple audio and video files to accommodate different browsers and how to properly resize videos.

In the next chapter, we will be examining how to create HTML tables. We will also style those tables using CSS for a better looking website.

List of Tags, Styles and terminologies introduced

Tag, Style or Terminology	Definition
Links	An element that allows a user to move from one website to another or navigate a single website.
\<a\>	The anchor tag, which begins a link.
\<a href=""\>	href is an attribute to the anchor tag that indicates a hypertext reference, which references a website or an anchor on a page.
\<a name=""\>	Name is an attribute of the anchor tag that creates an anchor to link to the position on the page.
CSS Pseudo-class	A way to alter a selector in CSS that changes an element depending on the state of the selector.
font-weight	A style property that allows you to alter the boldness of text content.

Chapter 6: Tables

Chapter Objectives:
•Students will be able to create tables using HTML.
•Students will be able to style tables in HTML.
•Students will be able to style tables using CSS.

6.1 Creating Tables with HTML

In this chapter, we will create tables via HTML and render some table border design within HTML and then with CSS. In the past, tables were used for the entire webpage's design and layout. Nowadays, design and layout are accomplished using CSS, while tables are used for presenting information or data in tabular form.

Creating tables in HTML is easy. The table is created with the **<table>** tag. It is broken into rows with the table row **<tr>** tag. Each cell in the table is represented by either a table heading tag **<th>** or table data tag **<td>**. Let's begin our first table. The heading tags will be: Player Name, Player Position and Batting Average. We create this using the <th> tags. The code should look as follows:

```
<tr><th>Player Name</th><th>Player Position</th><th>Batting
Average</th></tr>
```

This will display the heading all in one row. To add a little enhancement, let us surround the headings with borders. We do that by including **borders=** attribute after the opening table tag as follows:

```
<table border="value">
```

Let us now add the rest of the data in the table. To add more rows, we use the <tr> tag to surround the row, then each cell is introduced using the <td>. Therefore, the code for our next row is:

```
<tr><td>Todd Smith</td><td>Pitcher</td><td>.125</td></tr>
```

If you need a cell to span two rows, add the **rowspan=** attribute within the <td> tag of the cell that the attribute will span to. For example:

```
<td>Jamal Williams</td><td rowspan="2">Left Field</td><td>.312</td>
```

There is also a column span, that is, it spans two columns. The attribute is **colspan=** and the syntax is:

```
<td colspan="2">data cell</td>
```

Another tag used in tables is **<caption>** which can be used to place annotation for the table. The <caption> tag can be placed at the beginning or end of the table tag as long as it appears within the table tag.

Code Listing: HTML Tables

```
<?xml version="1.0" encoding="UTF-8"?>
<!DOCTYPE html PUBLIC "-//W3C//DTD XHTML 1.0 Strict//EN"
"http://www.w3.org/TR/xhtml1/DTD/xhtml1-strict.dtd">
<html xmlns="http://www.w3.org/1999/xhtml" xml:lang="en" lang="en">
<head>
    <title>Tables</title>
</head>
```

```
<body>
    <table>
        <tr>
            <th>Player Name</th><th>Player Position</th>
            <th>Batting Average</th>
        </tr>
        <tr>
            <td>Todd Smith</td><td colspan="2">Pitcher</td>
        </tr>
        <tr>
            <td>Fred Thomas</td><td>Catcher</td><td>.300</td>
        </tr>
        <tr>
            <td>Jamal Williams</td><td>Left Field</td><td>.312</td>
        </tr>
        <tr>
            <td>Tommy Thomas</td><td>Center Field</td><td>.256</td>
        </tr>
        <caption>Westport Little League All-Stars</caption>
    </table>
</body>
</html>
```

This is a complete table code sample and the next image shows how it will look in the browser. The table is still very plain and in the next section, CSS will be added to improve the look of our table.

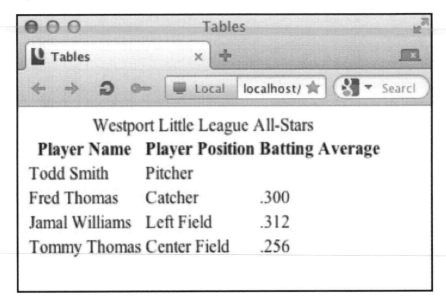

Questions for Review

1. What are tables used for when CSS is a part of your HTML?
a. Design and layout.
b. Displaying tabular information.
c. Organizing headers.

d. Comments.

2. What tag do you use to start a table?
a. <create table>
b. <start table>
c. <table>
d. <move table>

3. What tag is used to start a table row?
a. <tr>
b. table row>
c. <t>
d. <r>

4. Which is the correct attribute syntax if you want to create a border for your table?
a. <"border"=1>
b. <border>
c. <table =1>
d. <table Border="1">

5. What tag creates cells within a table?
a. <tr>
b. <th>
c. <td>
d. <t>

Lab Activity

Using an HTML5 document, create a table that will produce an output exactly like the image shown below using table properties introduced in this subchapter:

Sport Name	Number of Players per Team	Points to Win
Hockey		
Football		
Baseball	9	
Basketball	10-20, 5 on court	maximum points earned against opponent
Volleyball	6	
Water Polo	7-6 field players and 1 goal player	
Rowing	varies on type of boat	first to reach goal
Rugby League	13	
Cricket	11	
Lacrosse	10	

Extra task: Fill in missing information in the blank cells and update the following codes.

Lab Solution

```
<!DOCTYPE html>
<html>
<head>
    <title>Tables</title>
</head>
<body>
    <table border="5">
        <tr>
        <th>Sport Name</th><th>Number of Players per
        Team</th><th>Points to Win</th>
        </tr>
        <tr class="odd">
            <td>Hockey</td><td></td><td></td>
        </tr>
        <tr class="even">
            <td>Football</td><td></td><td></td>
        </tr>
        <tr class="odd">
            <td>Baseball</td><td>9</td><td></td>
        </tr>
```

```html
        <tr class="even">
        <td>Basketball</td><td>10-20, 5 on court</td><td>maximum
        points earned against opponent</td>
        </tr>
        <tr class="odd">
            <td>Volleyball</td><td>6</td><td></td>
        </tr>
        <tr class="even">
            <td>Water Polo</td><td>7-6 field players and 1 goal
player</td><td></td>
        </tr>
        <tr class="odd">
            <td>Rowing</td><td>varies on type of boat</td><td>first
to reach goal</td>
        </tr>
        <tr class="even">
            <td>Rugby League</td><td>13</td><td></td>
        </tr>
        <tr class="odd">
            <td>Cricket</td><td>11</td><td></td>
        </tr>
        <tr class="even">
            <td>Lacrosse</td><td>10</td><td></td>
        </tr>
        <caption>Popular Team Sports</caption>
    </table>
</body>
</html>
```

6.2 Styling Tables with CSS

In this section, we will add inline CSS to improve the look of our table.

First, let us introduce a border around the table. To add the surrounding borders, include the attribute **border: 2px solid #0000AA** right under the table selector element found within the style tags, then end the code line with a semi-colon (;). The code should look like this:

```
<style type="text/css">
      table
      {
        border: 2px solid #0000AA;
      }
```

This puts a border around the table, but not surrounding each cell. To put borders around each cell, add selector elements **th** and **td** in the style tag with a border attribute of its own. Refer to the code below to see how this can be accomplished:

```
<style type="text/css">
           table
           {
           border: 2px solid #0000AA;
           }

           th, td
           {
           border: 1px solid #0000AA;
           }
```

The code line shown in bold will create the border that surrounds each cell. Notice, however, that the border style displayed shows a double-lined border. This can be modified and collapsed by including the **border-collapse** attribute in the table styles. This is how the code should progress by now:

```
<style type="text/css">
           table
           {
           border: 2px solid #0000AA;
           border-collapse: collapse;
           }

           th, td
           {
           border: 1px solid #0000AA;
           }
```

Another way we can give our table an interesting look is by making it render alternate background colors between rows. Let's start with giving the header a black background and white text. Then, let us apply odd and even **class** attribute in each of the table rows opening tag. The class attribute syntax is as follows:

```
<tr class="odd">    or    <tr class="even">
```
The code should now be:

```
<style type="text/css">
        table
        {
        border: 2px solid #0000AA;
        border-collapse: collapse;
        }
        th, td
        {
        border: 1px solid #0000AA;
        }

        th
        {
        background-color: black;
        color: white;
        }
```

CSS class style may now be included. Begin a class with a dot so that CSS will not interpret it as a selector. Start with either the **.odd** or **.even** class. Here is how the code should look:

```
<style type="text/css">
        table
        {
        border: 2px solid #0000AA;
        border-collapse: collapse;
        }

        th, td
        {
        border: 1px solid #0000AA;
        }

        th
        {
background-color: black;
color: white;
        }
        .odd
        {
        background-color: black;
        color: white;
        }
.even
        {
        background-color: rgb(215,215,215)
         }
```

The font-type can also be set for the entire table or row. We can change the table header and table data fonts to display different fonts using **font-family: "font name"** attribute. We can also change the font size using the **font-size: "font size value"** attribute. Should you want to align the texts, the attribute to use is **text-align: "alignment value"**. Refer to the code below for a clearer grasp on the idea:

```
<style type="text/css">
        table
        {
```

```
border: 2px solid #0000AA;
border-collapse: collapse;
}
 th, td
{
border: 1px solid #0000AA;
font-family: arial;
font-size: .8em;
text-align: left;
}
th
{
background-color: black;
color: white;
}
.odd
{
background-color: black;
color: white;
}
.even
{
background-color:rgb(215,215,215)
}
```

Another styling you can do is setting the width of a table. There are different ways to change the width; one is by setting the table by means of pixel measure. The attribute to use is **width: "pixel size value";** next is by setting it to a percentage of the browser window, syntax is **width: "number%"**. This must be placed inside the table style selector. Remember that with percentage setting selected the table will always adjust to the size of the browser window. Refer to the following code to see exactly how width attribute is included:

```
<style type="text/css">
        table
        {
        border: 2px solid #0000AA;
        border-collapse: collapse;
        width: 400px;
        }
        th, td
        {
        border: 1px solid #0000AA;
        font-family: arial;
        font-size: .8em;
        text-align: left;
        }
        th
        {
        background-color: black;
        color: white;
        }

        .odd
        {
        background-color: black;
        color: white;
        }
```

```
.even
{
background-color:rgb(215,215,215)
color:
}
```

Styling your caption is also easy and enhances the look of the table. To change the placement of your caption, the **caption-side** attribute is used. Fonts can be changed using the font-family attribute and the size, with font-size attribute. Background color can also be changed to set the caption apart from the rest of the table. By default, captions don't have borders around them, but they can be surrounded by borders.

Here is the complete code that includes caption tags and styling. Observe how the table is styled and how the code is used. All sections that introduce caption use are made bold to emphasize. Notice the use of RGB method to set the table row background in different shades of grey. Refer to the following code listing and the expected output/display in the browser.

Code Listing: Styling Tables

```
<?xml version="1.0" encoding="UTF-8"?>
<!DOCTYPE html PUBLIC "-//W3C//DTD XHTML 1.0 Strict//EN"
"http://www.w3.org/TR/xhtml1/DTD/xhtml1-strict.dtd">
<html xmlns="http://www.w3.org/1999/xhtml" xml:lang="en" lang="en">
<head>
    <title>Tables</title>
    <style type="text/css">
        table
        {
        border: 2px solid black;
        border-collapse: collapse;
        width: 400px;
        }
        th, td
        {
        border: 1px solid black;
        font-family: arial;
        font-size: .8em;
        text-align:left;
        }
        th
        {
        background-color: black;
        color: white;
        }
        .odd
        {
        background-color: rgb(215,215,215);
        }
        .even
        {
        background-color: rgb(245, 245, 245);
        }
        caption
        {
        font-family: arial;
        font-size: 1.3em;
```

```
                caption-side: top;
                }
        </style>

</head>
<body>
    <table>

        <tr>
            <th>Player Name</th><th>Player Position</th><th>Batting
                Average</th>
        </tr>
        <tr class="odd">
            <td>Todd Smith</td><td colspan="2">Pitcher</td>
        </tr>
        <tr class="even">
            <td>Fred Thomas</td><td>Catcher</td><td>.300</td>
        </tr>
        <tr class="odd">
            <td>Jamal Williams</td><td>Left Field</td><td>.312</td>
        </tr>
        <tr class="even">
            <td>Tommy Thomas</td><td>Center Field</td><td>.256</td>
        </tr>
        <tr class="odd">
            <td>Phillip Zachary</td><td>1st Base</td><td>.309</td>
        </tr>
        <tr class="even">
            <td>Marc Patterson</td><td>2nd Base</td><td>.415</td>
        </tr>
        <tr class="odd">
            <td>Bryan Dill</td><td>3rd Base</td><td>.387</td>
        </tr>
        <tr class="even">
            <td>Nick Terry</td><td>Right Field</td><td>.289</td>
        </tr>
        <caption>Westport Little League All-Stars</caption>
    </table>
  </body>
</html>
```

This is how the table will look when viewed in the browser:

Questions for Review

1. What attribute do you use to put a border around the table in CSS?
a.{ table {border: enter attributes }
b. border {attributes: ; }
c. table {attributes: ; }
d. table {line:enter attributes ; }

2. How would you create an attribute that would make the background of a table header black and the text white?
a. <tr> { background-color=black; color=white }
b. <th> { background-color: black; color: white }
c. <td> { background-color: black; color: white }
d. <table> { background-color=black; color=white }

3. How do you set the width of the table to be a constant 70 percent of the browser window in CSS?
a. {table width:70px; }
b. tablewidth: 70px;}
c. {table width: 70 percent; }
d. {table width: 70%;}

Chapter 6 Lab Exercises

1) Create a correct and standard-compliant XHTML basic document structure. Inside the **<title>** element place the text **Lab 6: Tables**.

2) Just below your opening <body> tag, insert an **<h1>** element with the text "**New York Yankees Pitching Staff**"

3) Use the spreadsheet below and, using <table>, <tr>, <th> and <td> tags, recreate the spreadsheet as an HTML table.

4) Using CSS, style the table according to the following specifications:

Grid Lines: All table grid lines should be **visible and collapsed**. Grid lines should be **black.**
Font: The table should be displayed in **Verdana**
Font Size: Headings should be displayed at **.8em and bold**. Table **data** should be displayed **at .7 em**.
Color: The **table heading row** should have a **deep blue background and white text**. Odd rows will have a white background with deep blue text. Even rows will have a deep blue background with white text.
Padding: All cells should have 2px of passing around the content.

NO.	NAME	POS	AGE	BIRTH PLACE	SALARY
38	Luis Ayala	RP	33	Los Mochis, Mexico	$650,000
66	Andrew Brackman	RP	25	Cincinnati, OH	N/A
34	A.J. Burnett	SP	34	North Little Rock, AR	$16,500,000
40	Bartolo Colon	SP	38	Altamira, Dominican Republic	$900,000
36	Freddy Garcia	SP	35	Caracas, Venezuela	$1,500,000
65	Phil Hughes	SP	25	Mission Viejo, CA	$2,700,000
70	George Kontos	RP	26	Lincolnwood, IL	N/A
22	Aaron Laffey	RP	26	Cumberland, MD	$431,600
48	Boone Logan	RP	27	San Antonio, TX	$1,200,000
64	Hector Noesi	RP	24	Esperanza, Dominican Republic	N/A
47	Ivan Nova	SP	24	San Cristobal, Dominican Republic	$432,900
41	Scott Proctor	RP	34	Stuart, FL	N/A
42	Mariano Rivera	RP	41	Panama City, Panama	$14,911,701
30	David Robertson	RP	26	Birmingham, AL	$460,450
52	CC Sabathia	SP	31	Vallejo, CA	$24,285,714
29	Rafael Soriano	RP	31	San Jose, Dominican Republic	$9,000,000
61	Raul Valdes	RP	33	Havana, Cuba	N/A
53	Cory Wade	RP	28	Indianapolis, IN	N/A

Lab Solution

```
<?xml version="1.0" encoding="UTF-8"?>
<!DOCTYPE html PUBLIC "-//W3C//DTD XHTML 1.0 Strict//EN"
"http://www.w3.org/TR/xhtml1/DTD/xhtml1-strict.dtd">
<html xmlns="http://www.w3.org/1999/xhtml" xml:lang="en" lang="en">
<html>
    <head>
```

```html
        <title>Sample Table</title>
        <style type="text/css">
            table
            {
                border: 2px solid black;
                border-collapse: collapse;
                width: 800px;
            }
            th, td
            {
                border: 1px solid black;
                font-family: verdana;
                text-align: left;
            }
            th
            {
                font-size: .8em;
                background-color: blue;
                color: white;
            }
            td
            {
                font-size: .7em;
            }

            h1
            {
                font-family: verdana;
                text-align: center;
            }

            .even
            {
                background-color: blue;
                color: white;
            }

            .odd
            {
                background-color: white;
                color: blue;
            }
        </style>
    </head>
    <body>
        <h1>New York Yankees Pitching Staff</h1>
        <table>
            <tr>
<th>NO.</th><th>NAME</th><th>POS</th><th>AGE</th><th>BIRTH
PLACE</th> <th>SALARY</th>
            </tr>
            <tr class="odd">
                <td>38</td><td>Luis Ayala</td> <td>RP</td>
<td>33</td> <td>Los Mochis,Mexico</td> <td>$650,000</td>
            </tr>
            <tr class="even">
                <td>66</td> <td>Andrew Brackman</td> <td>RP</td>
<td>25</td><td>Cincinnati,OH</td><td>N/A</td>
            </tr>
            <tr class="odd">
```

```
                    <td>34</td><td>A.J. Burnett</td> <td>SP</td>
<td>34</td><td>North Little Rock, AZ</td><td>$16,000,000</td>
            </tr>
            <tr class="even">
                    <td>40</td><td>Bartolo Colon</td> <td>SP</td>
<td>38</td><td>Altamira, Dominican Republic</td><td>$900,000</td>
            </tr>
            <tr class="odd">
                    <td>36</td><td>Freddy Garcia</td> <td>SP</td>
<td>35</td><td>Caracas, Venezuela</td><td>$1,500,000</td>
            </tr>
            <tr class="even">
                    <td>65</td><td>Phil Hughes</td> <td>SP</td>
<td>25</td><td>Mission Viejo, CA</td><td>$2,700,000</td>
            </tr>
            <tr class="odd">
                    <td>70</td><td>George Kontos</td>
<td>RP</td><td>26</td><td>Lincolwood, IL</td><td>N/A</td>
            </tr>
            <tr class="even">
                    <td>22</td><td>Aaron Lafey</td>
<td>RP</td><td>26</td><td>Cumberland, MD</td td>$431,000</td>
            </tr>
            <tr class="odd">
                    <td>48</td><td>Boone Logan</td>
<td>RP</td><td>27</td><td>San Antonio, TX</td><td>$1,200,000</td>
            </tr>
            <tr class="even">
                    <td>64</td><td>Hector Noesi</td> <td>RP</td>
<td>24</td><td>Esperanza, Dominican Republic</td><td>N/A</td>
            </tr>
            <tr class="odd">
                    <td>47</td><td>Ivan Nova</td> <td>SP</td>
<td>24</td> <td>San Cristobal, Dominican Republic</td>
<td>$432,900</td>
            </tr>
            <tr class="even">
                    <td>41</td><td>Scott
Proctor</td><td>RP</td><td>34</td><td>Stuart, FL</td><td>N/A</td>
            </tr>
            <tr class="odd">
                    <td>42</td><td>Mariano Rivera</td> <td>RP</td>
<td>41</td><td>Panam City, Panama</td><td>$14,911,701</td>
            </tr>
            <tr class="even">
                    <td>30</td><td>David Robertson</td>
<td>RP</td><td>26</td><td>Birmingham, AL</td><td>$40,450</td>
            </tr>
            <tr class="odd">
                    <td>52</td><td>CC Sabathia</td>
<td>SP</td><td>31</td><td>Vallejo, CA</td><td>$24,28,714</td>
            </tr>
            <tr class="even">
                    <td>29</td><td>Rafael Soriano</td> <td>RP</td>
<td>31</td><td>San Jose, Dominican Republic</td>
<td>$9,000,000</td>
            </tr>
            <tr class="odd">
                    <td>61</td><td>Raul Valdez</td>
<td>RP</td><td>33</td><td>Havana, Cuba</td><td>N/A</td>
```

```
            </tr>
            <tr class="even">
                <td>53</td><td>Cory Wade</td>
<td>RP</td><td>28</td><td>Indianopolis, IN</td><td>N/A</td>
            </tr>
        </table>
    </body>
</html>
```

Solution viewed in browser:

New York Yankees Pitching Staff

NO.	NAME	POS	AGE	BIRTH PLACE	SALARY
33	Luis Ayala	RP	33	Los Mochis, Mexico	$650,000
66	Andrew Brackman	RP	25	Cincinnati,OH	N/A
34	A.J. Burnett	SP	34	North Little Rock, AZ	$16,000,000
40	Bartolo Colon	SP	38	Altamira, Dominican Republic	$900,000
36	Freddy Garcia	SP	35	Caracas, Venezuela	$1,500,000
65	Phil Hughes	SP	25	Mission Viejo, CA	$2,700,000
70	George Kontos	RP	26	Lincolwood, IL	N/A
22	Aaron Lafey	RP	26	Cumberland, MD	$431,000
48	Boone Logan	RP	27	San Antonio, TX	$1,200,000
64	Hector Noesi	RP	24	Esperanza, Dominican Republic	N/A
47	Ivan Nova	SP	24	San Cristobal, Dominican Republic	$432,900
41	Scott Proctor	RP	34	Stuart, FL	N/A
42	Mariano Rivera	RP	41	Panam City, Panama	$14,911,701
30	David Robertson	RP	26	Birmingham, AL	$40,450
52	CC Sabathia	SP	31	Vallejo, CA	$24,28,714
29	Rafael Soriano	RP	31	San Jose, Dominican Republic	$9,000,000
61	Raul Valdez	RP	33	Havana, Cuba	N/A
53	Cory Wade	RP	28	Indianopolis, IN	N/A

Chapter 6 Summary

In Chapter 6 we discussed how tables are created in HTML, cited their purpose and use, and introduced basic table design.

Use of CSS in designing tables was presented and our discussion covered fonts, borders, class and caption styling.

The next chapter will discuss how to gather information from the user via HTML textbox elements.

List of Tags, Styles and terminologies Introduced

Tag, Style or Terminology	Definition
<table>	A tag that begins a table in HTML.
<tr>	A tag that defines a row in the table.
<th>	A tag that defines a table heading.
<td>	A tag that defines a cell in a table.
rowspan="xxx"	An attribute that defines how many rows a cell will use.
colspan="xxx"	An attribute that defines how many columns a cell will use.
<caption>	A tag that adds a caption to the table.
class="xxx"	A selector that styles the elements that are defined as the specified class.
caption-side:	Position of caption.

Chapter 7: HTML Forms

Chapter Objectives
- Students will be able to create HTML forms.
- Students will be able to implement radio buttons and checkbox elements.
- Students will be able to use HTML5 form elements.
- Students will be able to create multi-select form elements.

7.1 Creating Text Form Elements

In this chapter we are going to generate HTML forms. Forms allow users to input data or information into an application or website for processing. Forms are also one of the factors that affect whether users do what you want them to do in a specific webpage.

To create forms you use the **<form>** tag. The <form> tag has two attributes that are regularly used: action and method. The action attribute tells the form where to send the information to be processed. The information is usually sent to a PHP form or another back end language. Since this course doesn't deal with PHP, you can instead put **"#"** in the action attribute. Method, on the other hand, defines how the data will be sent. The two values for sending data are get and post. Get is less common and appends information the user types to the URL as a query string and passes it to the page indicated in action. Get is not a secure way of passing information because the information appears in the URL. Post places all the information in an array and passes it to the indicated page. It is considered more secure than Get. The complete code for an open form tag is:

```
<form action="#" method="post">
```

To make the HTML form look neat and properly laid out, place it inside a table, making each input element part of a table row. This technique will lessen the use of break tags <br> and spaces in aligning the texts.

The first **input type** is the **text** input:

```
<input type="text"
```

Then give the tag a name. This is how it will be referred to when passed to the server. In this case, our tag is named "first". The tag will now look like this:

```
<input type="text" name="first"
```

If you are also using Javascript, you would want to make sure the tag also contains an id for the Javascript to use. The id value can be the same as the name but it determines how the information is grabbed using Javascript. The tag now looks like this:

```
<input type="text" name="first" id="first" />
```

Another input type is **password**. Its difference is that instead of displaying what the user typed, each character is displayed as dots or asterisks. The entire tag now for the password should look something like this:

```
<input type="password" name="password" id="password" />
```

Once text entries can be filled out, what you will need next is the submit button. This button sends the information to the server depending on the content of the action attribute of the form tag. To create the submit button, use the input type **submit** tag:

```
<input type="submit" />
```

You can also change the text displayed on the button with the **value attribute**. The complete tag is:

```
<input type="submit" value="Send Info" />
```

Some forms will need a reset button to clear all entries in the form. The tag for the **reset button** would look like this:

```
<input type="reset" />
```

Refer to the following code listing which incorporates all the discussed form elements including buttons.

Code Listing: Creating a form

```
<?xml version="1.0" encoding="UTF-8"?>
<!DOCTYPE html PUBLIC "-//W3C//DTD XHTML 1.0 Strict//EN"
"http://www.w3.org/TR/xhtml1/DTD/xhtml1-strict.dtd">
<html xmlns="http://www.w3.org/1999/xhtml" xml:lang="en" lang="en">
<head>
<title>Creating a Form</title>
</head>
<body>
    <form action="#" method="post">
        <table>
            <tr>
                <td>First Name:</td>
                <td><input type="text" name="first"
id="first"/></td>
            </tr>
            <tr>
                <td>Last Name:</td>
                <td><input type="text" name="last" id="last"
/></td>
            </tr>
            <tr>
                <td>Password:</td>
                <td><input type="password" name="password"
id="password" /></td>
            </tr>
            <tr>
                <td><input type="reset" /></td>
                <td><input type="submit" value="Send Info" />
        </table>
    </form>
</body>
</html>
```

This is how the output would look when viewed in the browser:

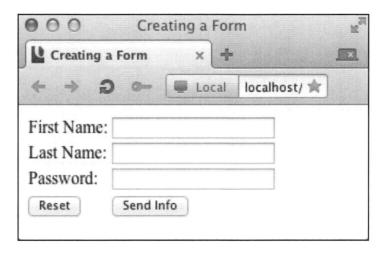

Questions for Review

1. Why are forms important to have on your website?
a. It's easier to manage the HTML with good forms.
b. It looks nicer.
c. Forms allow users to input information in the website for processing, especially if the website deals with exchange of information.
d. It makes the users do what the designers of the website want them to do.

2. What form tag attribute is required for forms to work?
a. <form action="#" method="">
b. <form go="#" method="">
c. <form action="#" attribute="#">
d. <form go="#" method="">

3. How do you create a text form that changes the input to dots and asterisks?
a. <input type="dot"
b. <input type="asterisk"
c. <input type="text"
d. <input type="password"

Lab Activity

Create an XHTML document and type the following code:

```
<?xml version="1.0" encoding="UTF-8"?>
<!DOCTYPE html PUBLIC "-//W3C//DTD XHTML 1.0 Strict//EN"
"http://www.w3.org/TR/xhtml1/DTD/xhtml1-strict.dtd">
<html xmlns="http://www.w3.org/1999/xhtml" xml:lang="en" lang="en">
<head>
<title>Creating a Form</title>
</head>
<body>
    <form action="#" method="post">
        <table>
            <tr>
                <td>First Name:</td>
                <td><input type="text" name="first"
id="first"/></td>
            </tr>
            <tr>
                <td>Last Name:</td>
                <td><input type="text" name="last" id="last"
/></td>
            </tr>
            <tr>
                <tr>
                    <td>Middle Initial</td>
                    <td><input type="text" name="middle" id="middle"
/></td>
                    <td>Password:</td>
                    <td><input type="password" name="password"
id="password" /></td>
                </tr>
                <tr>
                    <td><input type="reset" /></td>
                    <td><input type="submit" value="Send Info" />
            </table>
    </form>
</body>
</html>
```

Your output should look like this when viewed in the browser:

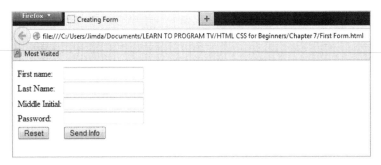

7.2 Creating Radio Button and Checkbox Elements

This section discusses the two input types that the user clicks in the form. These are **radio buttons** and **checkboxes**.

A **radio button** is an input type that lets the user select one option from two or more distinct choices. A good example would be gender. Working from the form we created previously, we will add a row for gender and populate it with radio buttons.

When a radio button is used, at least two buttons need to be created to select a choice. For gender button, there must be one button for male and another button for female. The form names will be the same but their values differ. To the right of the tag is the name of the value. The tag for the male option is:

```
<input type="radio" value="male" name=gender"> Male
```

The female radio button is placed on the same line.

```
<input type="radio" value="female" name=gender"> Female
```

Let's add another radio button for age. Let us make age values a range so that there will be multiple entries for this selection. The range values can be from any range combination provided each differs from one another. Let us use these ranges:

```
<input type="radio" value="0" name=age"> Under 18 <br/>
<input type="radio" value="1" name=age"> 19-39 <br/>
```

You can add more options for these, but remember that radio buttons only allow one choice so care must be observed when applying radio buttons.

Now let us go to checkboxes. Creation of checkboxes is similar to radio buttons. The only difference is that the input type is now "checkbox" instead of "radio" and it allows users to select multiple options. In the following code listing sample, two of the checkbox tags used are as follows:

```
<input type="checkbox" value="journey" name="bands"/> Journey<br/>
<input type="checkbox" value="reo" name="bands"/>REO<br/>
```

Putting these tag and element fragments together in a complete code we have:

Code Listing: Radio Button and Checkbox Elements

```
<?xml version="1.0" encoding="UTF-8"?>
<!DOCTYPE html PUBLIC "-//W3C//DTD XHTML 1.0 Strict//EN"
"http://www.w3.org/TR/xhtml1/DTD/xhtml1-strict.dtd">
<html xmlns="http://www.w3.org/1999/xhtml" xml:lang="en" lang="en">
<head>
<title>Creating a Form</title>
</head>
<body>
```

```
<form action="#" method="post">
    <table>
        <tr>
            <td>First Name:</td>
            <td><input type="text" name="first"
id="first"/></td>
        </tr>
        <tr>
            <td>Last Name:</td>
            <td><input type="text" name="last" id="last"
/></td>
        </tr>
        <tr>
            <td>Password:</td>
            <td><input type="password" name="password"
id="password" /></td>
        </tr>
        <tr>
            <td>Gender:</td>
            <td>
                <input type="radio" value="male"
name="gender">Male
                <input type="radio" value="female"
name="gender">Female
            </td>
        </tr>
        <tr>
            <td valign="top">Age Range:</td>
            <td>
                <input type="radio" value="0" name="age"
/>Under 18<br/>
                <input type="radio" value="1" name="age" />19-
39<br/>
                <input type="radio" value="2" name="age" />40-
59<br/>
                <input type="radio" value="3" name="age" />Over
60<br/>
            </td>
        </tr>
        <tr>
            <td valign="top">Bands you like:</td>
            <td>
                <input type="checkbox" value="journey"
name="bands"/>Journey<br/>
                <input type="checkbox" value="reo"
name="bands"/>REO Speedwagon<br/>
                <input type="checkbox" value="survivor"
name="bands"/>Survivor<br/>
                <input type="checkbox" value="heart"
name="bands"/>Heart<br/>
            </td>
        </tr>
        <tr>
            <td><input type="reset" /></td>
            <td><input type="submit" value="Send Info" />
    </table>
</form>
</body>
</html>
```

This is how the form will look when viewed in a browser. For gender, the user can only select male or female, as well as only one age range. However, for the band they can select as many bands as they like.

Questions for Review

1. If a radio button has to be created for a "yes" answer as part of the group "Question", what would be the correct tag?
a. <input type="radio" name="Question" /> Yes
b. <input type="radio" value="yes" name="Question" /> Yes
c. <input type="button" name="Question" /> Yes
d. <input type="button" value="yes" name="Question" /> Yes

2. What tag is used to create a checkbox?
a. <input type="box"
b. <input type="checkbox"
c. <input type="check"
d. input type="text"

3. What is the difference between radio buttons and checkboxes in HTML?
a. Radio buttons allow you to select multiple items, checkboxes only one.
b. Checkboxes allow you to select only two items and radio buttons only one.
c. Checkboxes allow you to select multiple items and radio buttons only one.

d. There is no difference between them.

Lab Activity

Type the following code and view your output.

```
<?xml version="1.0" encoding="UTF-8"?>
<!DOCTYPE html PUBLIC "-//W3C//DTD XHTML 1.0 Strict//EN"
"http://www.w3.org/TR/xhtml1/DTD/xhtml1-strict.dtd">
<html xmlns="http://www.w3.org/1999/xhtml" xml:lang="en" lang="en">
<head>
    <title>Creating Form</title>
</head>
<body>
    <form action="#" method="post">
        <table>
          <tr>
            <td>First name:</td>
            <td><input type="text" name="first" id="first"/></td>
          </tr>
          <tr>
            <td>Last Name:</td>
            <td><input type="text" name="last" id="last"/></td>
          </tr>
          <tr>
          <tr>
            <td>Middle Initial:</td>
            <td><input type="middle" name="middle" id="middle"
                /></td>
          </tr>
            <td>Password:</td>
            <td><input type="password" name="password"
                id="password" /></td>
          </tr>
          <tr>
            <td>Gender:</td>
            <td>
              <input type="radio" value="male" name="gender">Male
              <input type="radio" value="female"
                name="gender">Female
            </td>
          </tr>
          <tr>
            <td valign="top">Bands you like:</td>
            <td>
              <input type="checkbox" value="journey"
                name="bands"/>Journey<br/>
              <input type="checkbox" value="reo" name="bands"/>REO
                Speedwagon<br/>
              <input type="checkbox" value="survivor"
                name="bands"/>Survivor<br/>
            </td>
          </tr>
          <tr>
            <td><input type="reset" /></td>
            <td><input type="submit" value="Send Info" /></td>
          </tr>
        </table>
```

```
        </form>
    </body>
</html>
```

Your output should look like this when viewed in a browser:

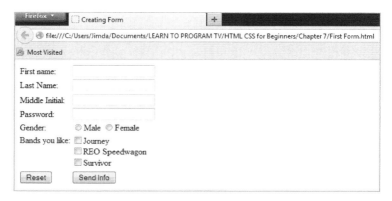

7.3 New HTML5 Form Elements

In this section we are going to discuss form elements that are included in HTML5. Keep in mind that many of these elements will not yet work with current browser settings and browser results are different. HTML5 will not be the standard HTML format until 2014.

HTML5 has the document declaration standard:

```
<!DOCTYPE html>
```

To work on forms with HTML5, two form attributes are needed, **action** and **method:**

```
<form action="#" method="post">
```

There are several new elements that come with HTML5; they are **color, date, time, tel, email and number**. Most of these elements are not yet supported by regular browsers at the time of this writing, but Opera has decent implementations of these elements and they can already be viewed using this browser.

The input element **type="color"** gives out a selection box that has a palette of different colors the user may select. Its tag is:

```
<input type="color" name="color" />
```

The **type="date"** element, on the other hand, brings out a widget type of calendar where the user may select a specific date and year. Its tag is:

```
<input type="date" name="date" />
```

A variation of the "date" element is **type="time"**, but instead of a calendar, a digital clock-like text box is seen that has up and down arrows that scroll through different time inputs. Its tag is:

```
<input type="time" name="time" />
```

Two elements that are unique and are mostly implemented on mobile browsers that make use of a touch screen are **type="email"** and **type="tel"**. Type "email" utilizes a textbox where the @ sign is affixed; whereas the type "telephone" might have a telephone pad in it. These are optimized to ease input for the user. The tags are:

```
<input type="email" name="email" />
```

and:

```
<input type="tel" name="telephone" />
```

Number, on the other hand, has a specific function that may limit the input that can be placed into the text box. This is useful when limiting the occurrence of weird entries for age, or number of properties, and so on.

166

```
<input type="number" name="number" min="1" max="10" />
```

Note: **min="1"** will display a 1 as the minimum value for entry and 10 for **max="10"**.

Code Listing: HTML5 Form Elements

```html
<!DOCTYPE html>

<html>
<head>
    <title>Html 5 Form Element</title>
</head>

<body>
    <form action="#" method="post">
        Color:
        <input type="color" name="color"/>
        <br/>Date of Birth:
        <input type="date" name="dob" />
        <br/>Time of Appointment:
        <input type="time" name="timeOfAppointment"/>
        <br/>Email:
        <input type="email" name="email"/>
        <br/>Telephone:
        <input type="tel" name="telephone" />
        <br/>Age:
        <input type="number" name="age" min="0" max="115"/>
    </form>
</body>
</html>
```

This is how the form appears on some browsers. Keep in mind that not all browsers support HTML5 forms yet. Email and telephone forms aren't changed because this is not a mobile browser. On mobile browsers, the forms would bring up an optimized keyboard for mobile devices.

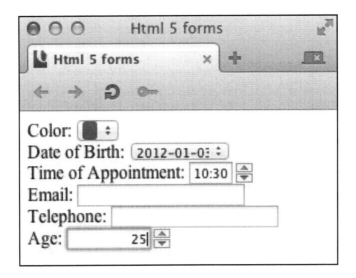

Questions for Review

1. What does the <input type="color" element create?
a. It allows the user to input their favorite color.
b. It changes the color of the code.
c. It allows the user to share colors.
d. It creates a box that allows a user to select a color.

2. What does the <input type="date" element create?
a. It gives the user an input box where they can input the date or open a calendar to select the date.
b. It is a text box where a user can write the date.
c. It allows the user to share when they were on a date last.
d. It allows you to stamp a date on the code.

3. What do the "min" and "max" attributes change in an input form?
a. They allow you to create minimum and maximum number data entries.
b. They allow you to create maximum color values.
c. They allow you to change the size of the table.
d. They allow a user to enter their birthday.

7.4 Creating Multi-Select Elements

This section discusses the **select** element known as a drop-down. This is commonly used for questions that would have multiple answers and might take up a lot of space in the browser if it is displayed altogether. A good example is country or state selection, which can have a long list of possible selections. The select element is used to optimize a small amount of space for the choices. **<select>** follows right under the basic form tag.

Say there is a poll question about which food the user likes best. Using select to accept the user's response, the tag would look like this:

```
<select name="food" size="7">
        <option value="continental">Continental</option>
        <option value="chinese">Chinese</option>
        <option value="italian">Italian</option>
        <option value="thai">Thai</option>
        <option value="indian">Indian</option>
        <option value="japanese">Japanese</option>
        <option value="vegetarian">Vegetarian</option>
</select>
```

Select has two other attributes that may improve how the drop-down behaves, **size=** and **multiple=**. Size determines how many rows the drop-down will allocate to display the choices while multiple allows two or more options to be selected from the list, just like a checkbox. Below is the tag:

```
<select name="food" size="7" multiple="multiple">
```

In the above attribute settings, the drop-down will have a maximum of seven choices and two or more entries could be selected from the list. Usually choices are taken from a database to avoid countless number options in the code.

Refer to the code listing shown for the multiple selection setting.

Code Listing: Multi-Select Elements

```
<?xml version="1.0" encoding="UTF-8"?>
<!DOCTYPE html PUBLIC "-//W3C//DTD XHTML 1.0 Strict//EN"
"http://www.w3.org/TR/xhtml1/DTD/xhtml1-strict.dtd">
<html xmlns="http://www.w3.org/1999/xhtml" xml:lang="en" lang="en">
<head>
    <title>Multiple Selection</title>
</head>
<body>
    <form action="#" method="post">
        Choose your favorite type of food:<br/>
        <select name="food" size="7" multiple="multiple">
            <option value="continental">Continental</option>
            <option value="chinese">Chinese</option>
            <option value="italian">Italian</option>
            <option value="thai">Thai</option>
            <option value="indian">Indian</option>
```

```
            <option value="japanese">Japanese</option>
            <option value="vegetarian">Vegetarian</option>
        </select>
    </form>
</body>
</html>
```

This is how our menu form will appear in the browser. Notice how all seven rows appear because we set the size attribute to 7.

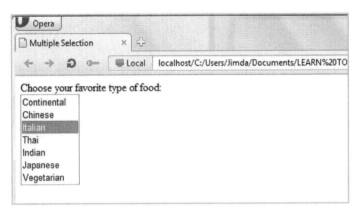

Questions for Review

1. What tag do you use to create your drop-down box?
a. <dropdown>
b. <list>
c. <form select>
d. <select>

2. If you wanted to make five items appear on the drop-down list at the same time, what element would you use?
a. dropdown=
b. size=
c. form=
d. select=

3. What element would you use to allow the user to select multiple items on the list?
a. select=multiple
b. dropdown=multiple
c. multiple=multiple
d. form=multiple

Lab Activity

Modify the following code so that the size is set to only display three choices, while increasing the number of overall choices to 10 by adding three more food varieties.

```
<?xml version="1.0" encoding="UTF-8"?>
<!DOCTYPE html PUBLIC "-//W3C//DTD XHTML 1.0 Strict//EN"
"http://www.w3.org/TR/xhtml1/DTD/xhtml1-strict.dtd">
<html xmlns="http://www.w3.org/1999/xhtml" xml:lang="en" lang="en">
<head>
    <title>Multiple Selection</title>
</head>
<body>
    <form action="#" method="post">
        Choose your favorite type of food:<br/>
        <select name="food" size=" " multiple="multiple">
            <option value="continental">Continental</option>
            <option value="chinese">Chinese</option>
            <option value="italian">Italian</option>
            <option value="thai">Thai</option>
            <option value="indian">Indian</option>
            <option value="japanese">Japanese</option>
            <option value="vegetarian">Vegetarian</option>


        </select>
    </form>
</body>
</html>
```

Your output should look like this when viewed in the browser:

Chapter 7 Lab Exercises

1) Create a standard-compliant XHTML basic document structure. Inside the **<title>** element place the text **Lab 7: Forms**.

2) Insert an **<h1>** element just below the opening <body> tag and use "Hospital Admission Information" as your element text.

3) Create a form that collects the following information. Use the form field and field types specified below. Lay out the form using a **<table>** and related elements so that it looks neat. Don't forget to label each of your form fields so your user knows what to place in each field. Use "#" for the value of your action and "post" as the method.

Form Field	Type of Field
Patient First Name	Text
Patient Last Name	Text
Patient Email Address	Text
Patient Phone Number	Text
Patient Street Address	Text
Patient City	Text
Patient State	Drop-Down
Patient Zip	Text
Patient Age	Number (Limited to entries between 0-115)
Patient DOB	Drop-down for Month and Day, Text for Year
Patient Gender	Radio Buttons for Male and Female
Patient Health History	Check Boxes for the following: Heart Attack Stroke Cancer Hypertension Depression COPD Other (Add Text Field for explanation)

4) Add submit and reset buttons to the bottom of the form.

5) Use CSS to make your <table> containing your form more visually pleasing.

Chapter Lab Solution

```
<html>
<head>
<title> Lab exercise for Chapter 7 </title>
</head>
<body>
<h1>Hospital Admission Information</h1>
  <form action="#" method="post">
```

```html
<table>
    <tr>
     <td>First Name:</td>
      <td>
        <input type="text" name="fname" id="fname" />
      </td>
    </tr>
    <tr>
      <td>Last Name:</td>
      <td>
        <input type="text" name="lname" id="lname" />
      </td>
    </tr>
    <tr>
      <td>Email Address:</td>
     <td>
        <input type="text" name="eadd" id="eadd" />
      </td>
    </tr>
    <tr>
      <td>Phone Number:</td>
     <td>
        <input type="text" name="phnum" id="phnum" />
      </td>
 </tr>
    <tr>
      <td>Street Address:</td>
      <td>
        <input type="text" name="address" id="address" />
     </td>
    </tr>
    <tr>
      <td>City:</td>
      <td>
        <input type="text" name="city" id="city" />
      </td>
    </tr>
    <tr>
      <td>State:</td>
      <td>
          <select>
            <option>State 1</option>
            <option>State 2</option>
            <option>State 3</option>
            <option>State 4</option>
            <option>State 5</option>
            <option>State 6</option>
            <option>State 7</option>
          </select>
      </td>
    </tr>
     <tr>
      <td>Zip:</td>
      <td>
          <input type="text" name="zip" id="zip" />
      </td>
     </tr>
     <tr>
      <td>Age:</td>
        <td>
```

```html
              <input type="number" name="city" id="city" min="0"
          max="115" />
        </td>
      </tr>
      <tr>
        <td>Date of Birth:</td>
        <td>
            <select name="dob">
              <option value="jan">1</option>
              <option value="feb">2</option>
              <option value="mar">3</option>
              <option value="apr">4</option>
              <option value="may">5</option>
              <option value="jun">6</option>
              <option value="jul">7</option>
              <option value="aug">8</option>
              <option value="sep">9</option>
             <option value="oct">10</option>
              <option value="nov">11</option>
              <option value="dec">12</option>
            </select> -
          <select>
<option value="1">1</option>
<option value="2">2</option>
<option value="3">3</option>
<option value="4">4</option>
<option value="5">5</option>
<option value="6">6</option>
<option value="7">7</option>
<option value="8">8</option>
<option value="9">9</option>
<option value="10">10</option>
<option value="11">11</option>
<option value="12">12</option>
<option value="13">13</option>
<option value="14">14</option>
<option value="15">15</option>
<option value="16">16</option>
<option value="17">17</option>
<option value="18">18</option>
<option value="19">19</option>
<option value="20">20</option>
<option value="21">21</option>
<option value="22">22</option>
<option value="23">23</option>
<option value="24">24</option>
<option value="25">25</option>
<option value="26">26</option>
<option value="27">27</option>
<option value="28">28</option>
<option value="29">29</option>
<option value="30">30</option>
<option value="31">31</option>
            </select> -
          <input type="text" name="year" id="year" />
        </td>
      <tr>
          <td>Gender:</td>
          <td>
            <input type="radio" name="gender" id="gender"
```

```
                    />Male</input>
                     <input type="radio" name="gender" id="gender"
                    />Female</input>
                    </td>
              </tr>
              <tr>
                  <td>Health History:</td>
                  <td>
                     <input type="checkbox" name="health"
value="hattack"
                    />Heart Attack</input><br/>
                     <input type="checkbox" name="health"
value="stroke"
                    />Stroke</input><br/>
                   <input type="checkbox" name="health" value="cancer"
                    />Cancer</input><br/>
                     <input type="checkbox" name="health" value="hyper"
                    />Hypertension</input><br/>
                     <input type="checkbox" name="health"
value="depression"
                    />Depression</input><br/>
                     <input type="checkbox" name="health" value="copd"
                    />COPD</input><br/>
                     Other<input type="text" name="health" id="health"
                    /></input>
                    </td>
              </tr>
              <tr>
                  <td><input type="submit" value="confirm" /></td>
                  <td><input type="reset" value="start over" /></td>
              </tr>
          </table>
      </form>
</body>
</html>
```

Chapter 7 Summary

In this chapter we learned how to use the HTML Forms. We were able to differentiate their input types and the attributes that go along with them—text, password, radio, checkbox, submit, reset, and select. We were able to create a simple form and integrate submit and reset buttons.

We were also able to use some of the new elements that are included in the HTML5 format: Color, Date, Time, Number, Email, and Tel. We have seen that not all browsers support these new elements yet.

In the next chapter we will discuss how to use the CSS box model. The CSS box model is a great way to lay out the content on your website in a professional manner.

List of Tags, Styles and Terminologies Introduced

Tag, Style or Terminology	Definition
<form>	The form tag which is used to create a form.
action="xxx"	An attribute that defines where the data from the form will be sent.
method="post"	An attribute that indicates how the data will be sent to the form.
<input>	The input tag which defines a field where users can enter data.
type="xxx"	An attribute which defines the type of form box displayed.
name="xxx"	An attribute which defines the name of the data being inputted.
id="xxx"	An attribute which defines the id of the data for use by other languages such as PHP and Javascript

Chapter 8: Understanding the CSS Box Model

Chapter Objectives
•Students will be able to understand the CSS box model.
•Students will be able to implement the CSS box model.
•Students will be able to adjust margin, padding and borders.

8.1 Understanding the Content Box Model

In this chapter we are going to review the CSS box model. The box model is a way of organizing the different units or parts of a web page. This model places your content into boxes or blocks. That content can be held in any type of container. For example, content can be contained in <p> tags or logical divisions. Anything that is a block level container follows the CSS box model.

In the middle of the CSS box model is the **content block**. This block may contain an image and/or text. Without any type of CSS, the box is the same width as the browser. Using the width property in CSS, the content block width can be changed simply by setting the width to a certain number of pixels or the percentage of the screen.

Just outside the content block is the padding. The **padding** is the space between the edge of the block and the content itself.

Surrounding the padding is the **border**. The border appears right outside of the padding. By using CSS the border width, pattern and color can all be controlled.

The final component of the box model is the **margin**. The margin is the space between your content block and the next content block or the edge of the browser window.

The margin area will take the background color of whatever element is behind it; this could be the page itself, whereas the border area will take on whatever color value is assigned to the border selector. The padding and content block areas will be colored together with the same rule color for the content block.

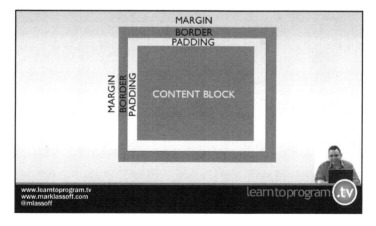

Most of the elements of the CSS box model can be changed using CSS. The next subchapter will show you how to do that.

Questions for Review

1. What is the CSS box model?
a. A model for putting your code in boxes.
b. A way of modifying form boxes.
c. A way of organizing the different units of a webpage.
d. A new way to add borders to information.

2. What is the padding in the box model?
a. The width of the box.
b. The edge of the box.
c. The content.
d. The space between the edge of the box and the content.

8.2 Working with Margin, Padding and Borders

In this section we will examine and learn how to control the various elements of the box model using CSS. To do this, we have created webpage content enclosed by a logical division element and given it the id, "box". By default, this content will appear as plain text in the browser. Using CSS, a great deal of control can be applied and will enhance the appearance of our content.

Let's try putting a border on our content to observe how it behaves in the browser.

Using inline CSS, right underneath the <title> tag, place the opening <style> tag followed by its attribute type="text/css". Next, indicate the box selector id by typing **#box**.

The hash tag (#) indicates that the selector is an id and is styled only once in HTML, whereas classes, preceded by a dot (.) can be styled multiple times.

Set the width of the box content to constrain the text; the style code is as follows:

```
<title>Box Model</title>
<style type="text/css">
        #box {
width: 375px;
                }
        </style>
```

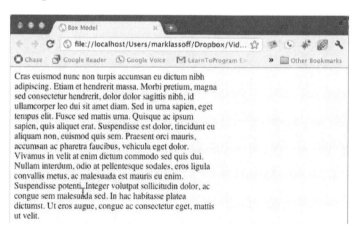

Now surround the box by a border; your code should now look like this:

```
<title>Box Model</title>
<style type="text/css">
        #box {
        width: 375px;
        border: 1px;
```

```
                    }
</style>
```

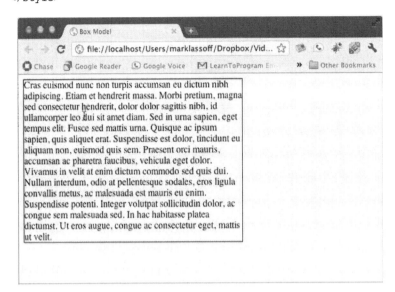

You will notice that there is space sitting between the edge of the browser window and our box content. Let us set the margin to zero:

```
<title>Box Model</title>
<style type="text/css">
        #box {
        width: 375px;
        border: 1px;
        margin: 0px;
                    }
 </style>
```

Setting the margin value to zero did not remove the margin, indicating that the gap is not caused by our content but by the window. To resolve this, what we need to do is include the **body selector** inside the style element preceding the box selector id and set the margin to zero from there. Our code should now be:

```
<title>Box Model</title>
<style type="text/css">
        body {
        margin: 0px;
}

        #box {
width: 375px;
border: 1px black solid;
</style>
```

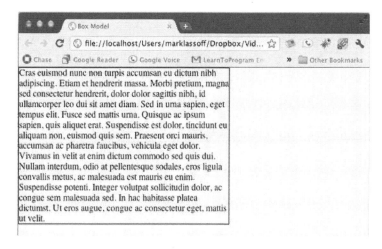

That removed the gap between the text box content and the browser.

To effectively see how margin settings behave, let us create a second body of text by adding another logical division and assigning it the value **id="box2"**:

```
<div id="box">
        (content)
</div>

<div id="box2">
        (content)
</div>
```

Let's have a different border color for the second box to distinguish them from one another. The CSS portion looks like this:

```
<style type="text/css">
body    {
        border: 0px;
        }
#box    {
        width: 375px;
        border: 1px black solid;
                                }
#box2{
        width: 375px;
        border: 1px red solid;
                                }
</style>
```

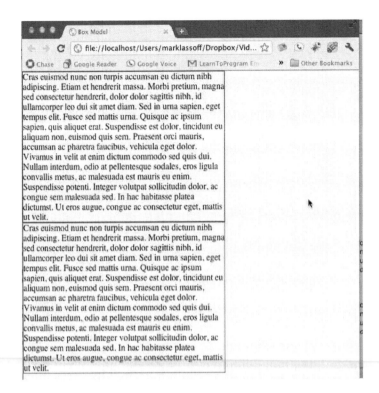

Variations of margin attribute settings are available. We can put margins separately for each content box and indicate the spacing in general or on each of the sides. The following margin attribute specifies the margin on each side of the content boxes.

```
#box    {
                width: 375px;
                border: 1px black solid;
                margin-bottom: 10px;
                margin-left: 10px;
        }
```

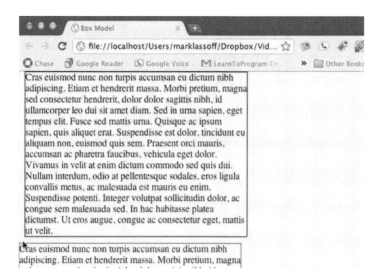

These margin settings can be done simply. Instead of using margin-top: -left:, -right:, -bottom:, we can use **margin: *px-value-top, px-value-rightside, px-value-bottom, px-value-leftside*** as in the code below:

```
margin: 5px, 100px, 100px, 5px;
```

This sets the top margin to 5px (margin: 5px); the right margin to 100px (100px,); the bottom margin to 100px (100px,) and the left margin to 5px (the last "5px" entry in the row).

Take note that when using "margin", the border margins you enter are in the sequence: top-right-bottom-left following a clockwise manner.

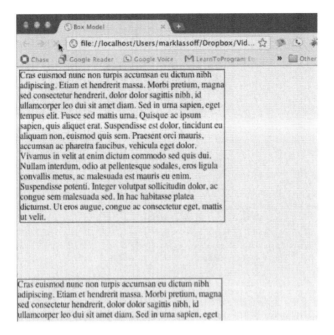

You can also have one value for "margin" which will give the same margin for all sides, meaning:

```
margin: 10px;
```

is the same as:

```
margin: 10px, 10px, 10px, 10px;
```

which tells the browser that the top margin has 10px, the right side margin has 10px, the bottom margin has 10px, and the left side margin has 10px.

Setting the padding is somewhat similar to setting the margin, only that while padding determines the space between the border and the content itself, it also works the same way as margin.

```
#box    {
                width: 375px;
                border: 1px black solid;
                margin-bottom 10px;
                margin-left 10px;
                padding: 10px;
                }
```

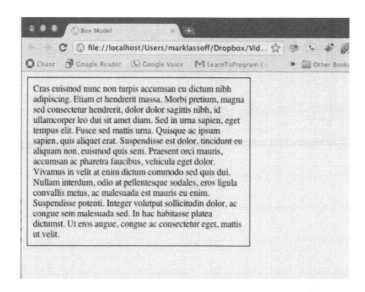

Another look you can apply to your box is setting its background color. Use the style attribute **background-color** to accomplish this. The padding color takes on the background color of the box but the margin takes on the background color of the page.

You also have the option to set the border to a variety of different styles. You can alter the area of the border, its type and color.

```
<style type="text/css">
body    {
        border: 0px;
        background-color: #aaaaaa;
                        }
                #box {
                width: 375px;
                border: 1px black solid;
                padding: 10px;
                background-color: #cccccc;
                }
```

Remember to take into consideration that the width of the padding, margins and borders are independent from the defined width of the division; meaning, the pixel sizes of each attribute is added to the total width specified for the division, for our example the total size of division is 375 + 10 + 10 + 1 + 1 = 397 pixels. So remember to finalize each attribute and content of the division before setting a fixed value for the width.

Code Listing: CSS Box Model

```
<?xml version="1.0" encoding="UTF-8"?>
<!DOCTYPE html PUBLIC "-//W3C//DTD XHTML 1.0 Strict//EN"
"http://www.w3.org/TR/xhtml1/DTD/xhtml1-strict.dtd">
<html xmlns="http://www.w3.org/1999/xhtml" xml:lang="en" lang="en">
<head>
```

```
<title>Box Model</title>
<style type="text/css">
    body    {
                margin: 0px;
                background-color: #aaaaaa;
            }

    #box    {
                width: 375px;
                border: 30px black solid;
                margin: 10px;
                padding: 10px;
                background-color: #cccccc;
            }
</style>
</head>
<body>
    <div id="box">

        Cras euismod nunc non turpis accumsan eu dictum nibh
adipiscing. Etiam et hendrerit massa. Morbi pretium, magna sed
consectetur hendrerit, dolor dolor sagittis nibh, id ullamcorper
leo dui sit amet diam. Sed in urna sapien, eget tempus elit. Fusce
sed mattis urna. Quisque ac ipsum sapien, quis aliquet erat.
Suspendisse est dolor, tincidunt eu aliquam non, euismod quis sem.
Praesent orci mauris, accumsan ac pharetra faucibus, vehicula eget
dolor. Vivamus in velit at enim dictum commodo sed quis dui. Nullam
interdum, odio at pellentesque sodales, eros ligula convallis
metus, ac malesuada est mauris eu enim. Suspendisse potenti.
Integer volutpat sollicitudin dolor, ac congue sem malesuada sed.
In hac habitasse platea dictumst. Ut eros augue, congue ac
consectetur eget, mattis ut velit.

    </div>
</body>
</html>
```

This is how our styled box looks when viewed in the browser:

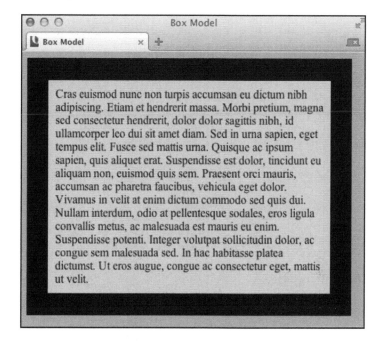

Questions for Review

1. In what order of directions does the margin attribute go?
a. Top, left, right, bottom.
b. Top, right, bottom, left.
c. Bottom, left, right, top.
d. Left, right, top, bottom.

2. What background color does the margin take on?
a. The background of the page.
b. The background of the box.
c. A blend of the background and the box.
d. The margin takes on no color.

3. What elements alter the width of your box?
a. Background color.
b. Border color.
c. Margins.
d. Padding and border.

4. Identify the function, purpose and, if appropriate, the output produced by each code fragment.
a. border: 1px black solid;
b. margin: 5px, 10px, 15px, 1px;
c. <div id="box">

d. padding: 10px
e. background-color: #aaaaaa;

5. In this activity, identify the elements of the box model.

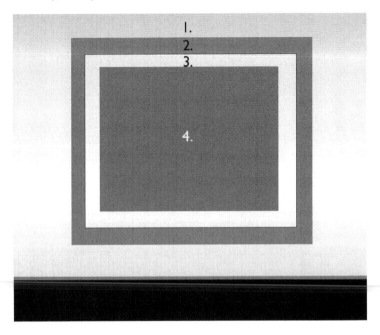

1.

2.

3.

4.

Chapter 8 Lab Exercises

Create a webpage that contains three content boxes. Set the following attributes in each of the boxes as follows:

	Padding:	Border:	Margin:	Content Color:
box 1:	10px	15px; green; solid	10px	default
box 2:	5px	15px; teal; groove	10px	default
box 3:	2px	15px; aqua; dotted	10px	default

Assume the number of divisions is one.

Lab Solution

```
<?xml version="1.0" encoding="UTF-8"?>
<!DOCTYPE html PUBLIC "-//W3C//DTD XHTML 1.0 Strict//EN"
"http://www.w3.org/TR/xhtml1/DTD/xhtml1-strict.dtd">
<html xmlns="http://www.w3.org/1999/xhtml" xml:lang="en" lang="en">
<head>
    <title>Box Model</title>
    <style type="text/css">
        body    {
                    margin: 10px;
                    background-color: #00ffff;
                }
        #box1   {
                    width: 365px;
                    border: 15px green solid;
                    margin: 10px;
                    padding: 10px;
                    background-color: #C0C0C0;
                }

        #box2   {
                    width: 370px;
                    border: 15px teal groove;
                    margin: 10px;
                    padding: 5px;
                    background-color: #008080;
                }

        #box3   {
                    width: 373px;
                    border: 15px aqua dotted;
                    margin: 10px;
                    padding: 2px;
                    background-color: #0000ff;
                }
    </style>
</head>
<body>
```

```
<div id="box1">
    Cras euismod nunc non turpis accumsan eu dictum nibh
adipiscing. Etiam et hendrerit massa. Morbi pretium, magna sed
consectetur hendrerit, dolor dolor sagittis nibh, id ullamcorper
leo dui sit amet diam. Sed in urna sapien, eget tempus elit. Fusce
sed mattis urna. Quisque ac ipsum sapien, quis aliquet erat.
    </div>

<div id="box2">
    Cras euismod nunc non turpis accumsan eu dictum nibh
adipiscing. Etiam et hendrerit massa. Morbi pretium, magna sed
consectetur hendrerit, dolor dolor sagittis nibh, id ullamcorper
leo dui sit amet diam. Sed in urna sapien, eget tempus elit. Fusce
sed mattis urna. Quisque ac ipsum sapien, quis aliquet erat.
    </div>    <div id="box3">
    Cras euismod nunc non turpis accumsan eu dictum nibh
adipiscing. Etiam et hendrerit massa. Morbi pretium, magna sed
consectetur hendrerit, dolor dolor sagittis nibh, id ullamcorper
leo dui sit amet diam. Sed in urna sapien, eget tempus elit. Fusce
sed mattis urna. Quisque ac ipsum sapien, quis aliquet erat.
    </div>
</body>
</html>
```

This is how the output will look when viewed in the browser:

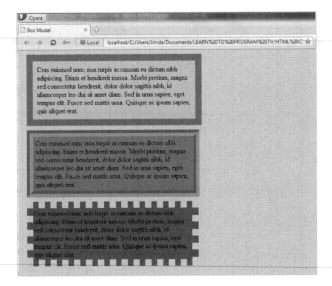

Chapter 8 Summary

In this chapter we discussed how the CSS box model is implemented. The CSS box model is used to create professional looking websites. You learned how to work with margin, padding and border elements to achieve the right look for your website.

The next and final chapter will discuss the differences and uses of inline versus block elements; how the float and clear attributes are used and how to create a navigation bar using CSS.

Tags, Styles and terminologies introduced

Tags, Style or terminology	Definition
CSS Box Model	A CSS design model, which contains the content of the HTML page in a neat and stylish way.
Margin	The area between the border and the rest of the webpage.
Content box	The area where the content is placed. The content can be anything from an image to text.
Border	A border that is situated between the padding and the margin.
Padding	The area between the content and the border.

Chapter 9: CSS Based Page Layout

Chapter Objectives
• Students will be able to understand the difference between inline vs. block level elements.
• Students will be able to position divs.
• Students will be able to implement float and clear attributes in the CSS box model.
• Students will be able to create a navigation bar using CSS.

9.1 Inline vs. Block Level Elements and Positioning Divs

In this chapter, we will talk about basic layout skills with HTML and CSS. CSS presents a standard-compliant layout process for a web page and it is essential to understand the underlying concepts and controls used in creating the box model, layout and divs position.

Let us start by having a document that already contains two divisions. Assign id values as div1 and div2. Enclose some text inside a paragraph tag in one of the divisions and some text portions in the same division inside a span tag. Create the CSS of the document selecting div1 and div2 as id. The following code will render a block level element:

```
<?xml version="1.0" encoding="UTF-8"?>
<!DOCTYPE html PUBLIC "-//W3C//DTD XHTML 1.0 Strict//EN"
"http://www.w3.org/TR/xhtml1/DTD/xhtml1-strict.dtd">
<html xmlns="http://www.w3.org/1999/xhtml" xml:lang="en" lang="en">
<head>
    <title>Inline div vs. Block div</title>
    <style type="text/css">
        #div1, #div2
            {
                font-family: arial;
                font-size: .8em;
                width: 400px;
                border:1px solid black;
            }
    </style>
</head>
<body>
    <div id="div1">
            Cras euismod nunc non turpis accumsan eu dictum nibh
adipiscing. Etiam et hendrerit massa. Morbi pretium, magna sed
consectetur hendrerit, dolor dolor sagittis nibh, id ullamcorper
leo dui sit amet diam. Sed in urna sapien, eget tempus elit. Fusce
sed mattis urna. Quisque ac ipsum sapien, quis aliquet erat.
    </div>
    <div id="div2">
            Cras euismod nunc non turpis accumsan eu dictum nibh
<span>adipiscing. Etiam et hendrerit massa. Morbi pretium,
</span>magna sed consectetur hendrerit, dolor dolor sagittis nibh,
<p>id ullamcorper leo dui sit amet diam. Sed in urna sapien, eget
tempus elit. Fusce sed mattis urna. Quisque ac ipsum sapien, quis
aliquet erat.</p>
    </div>
</body>
</html>
```

The above code will display the following output when viewed in the browser:

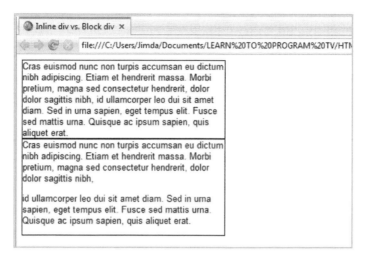

These elements by default are set to block positioning. If you want elements to be aligned horizontally, an "inline" attribute must be introduced first.

To introduce inline attributes, use the attribute modifier **display: inline** inside the style element for **#div1** and **p** selectors. The code listing below shows #div1 and p style elements contain the inline modifier code for inline level positioning while **span** selector shows the block level positioning using the modifier **display: block**.

```
#div1
    {
        display: inline;
    }
p
    {
        display: inline;
    }
span
    {
        display: block;
    }
```

Now the output becomes:

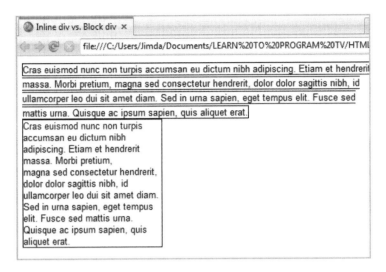

There you see the difference between block level and inline level positioning. Block versus inline is fairly easy to figure out and manipulate using CSS.

Now let us take a look at some different properties. We now know that we can set the width of an element through the **width:** *value* attribute. We can also set the height of an element via the attribute **height:** *value*. If the set height does not accommodate the whole text content, the excess or text overflow can be manipulated with the attribute **overflow:** *option*. Some options for overflow are: auto, scroll, visible and hidden.

Auto works in such a way that it only places a scroll bar whenever needed:

Scroll however attaches a scroll bar into the division to facilitate viewing of text or content by scrolling:

Visible makes the content visible including its overflow into other blocks:

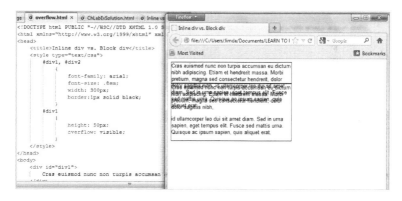

Hidden will not show the overflowing content, only the text or content that fits inside the block:

Another <div> property to discover is **position:** *value* which locks or controls the element being positioned anywhere in the document. There are several different values that can be set for the position. If you set the div to a **fixed** position, it will remain fixed on a particular location on the page and will stay in its position even when the user scrolls in the browser. If the position element is set to **absolute**, the element will be part of the page flow and will not stay on the page when the user scrolls down.

Following are image views where fixed and absolute positioning are shown:

Fixed:

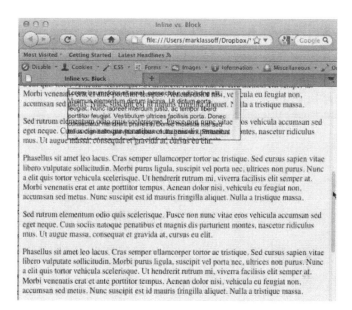

Absolute:

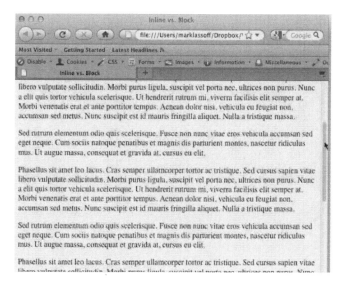

Code Listing: Inline vs. Block Elements

```
<?xml version="1.0" encoding="UTF-8"?>
<!DOCTYPE html PUBLIC "-//W3C//DTD XHTML 1.0 Strict//EN"
"http://www.w3.org/TR/xhtml1/DTD/xhtml1-strict.dtd">
<html xmlns="http://www.w3.org/1999/xhtml" xml:lang="en" lang="en">
```

```html
<head>
    <title>Inline vs. Block</title>
    <style type="text/css">
        #div1, #div2
            {
                font-family: arial;
                font-size: .8em;
                width: 350px;
                border: 1px solid black;
            }

        #div1
            {
                height: 100px;
                overflow: auto;
                position: absolute;
                top: 100px;
                left: 100px;
            }
        /*
        #div1
            {
                display: inline;
            }

        p   {
                display: inline;
            }
        span{
                display: block;
            }
        */
    </style>
</head>
<body>
    <div id="div1">
        Lorem ipsum dolor sit amet, consectetur adipiscing elit.
Vivamus elementum dictum lacinia. Ut dictum porta feugiat. Nunc
laoreet interdum justo, ac tempor libero porttitor feugiat.
Vestibulum ultrices facilisis porta. Donec consectetur hendrerit
pharetra. Donec molestie nisl sed tellus dignissim gravida aliquam
nulla hendrerit. Phasellus sed ante at neque faucibus eleifend.
Nulla lobortis ante vitae metus fermentum luctus. Suspendisse
luctus tincidunt tellus non blandit. Morbi congue vestibulum lectus
at imperdiet.
    </div>
    <!--
    <div id="div2">
        Phasellus sit amet leo lacus. Cras semper ullamcorper
tortor ac tristique. <span>Sed cursus sapien vitae libero vulputate
sollicitudin. Morbi purus ligula, suscipit vel porta nec, ultrices
non purus.</span> Nunc a elit quis tortor vehicula scelerisque. Ut
hendrerit rutrum mi, viverra facilisis elit semper at. Morbi
venenatis erat et ante porttitor tempus. Aenean dolor nisi,
vehicula eu feugiat non, accumsan sed metus. Nunc suscipit est id
mauris fringilla aliquet. Nulla a tristique massa. <p>Sed rutrum
elementum odio quis scelerisque. Fusce non nunc vitae eros vehicula
accumsan sed eget neque. Cum sociis natoque penatibus et magnis dis
parturient montes, nascetur ridiculus mus. Ut augue massa,
consequat et gravida at, cursus eu elit.</p>
```

```
    -->

    </div>
</body>
</html>
```

For simplicity in viewing the code output, div2 was *commented*, however it may be *uncommented* to see the effect of overflow with the two divisions.

Questions for Review

1. How does an inline element function?
a. It stays within the box.
b. It has no formatting.
c. It stays within the line and adjusts to the width of the browser.
d. It stays out of the line.

2. If you wanted to create a sentence or sentences within inline text that stayed within its own block, what tag would you use and what attribute would you give it?
a. The <p> tag and an inline attribute.
b. The <span> tag and a box attribute.
c. The <span> tag and an inline attribute.
d. The <p> tag and a box attribute.

3. What attribute deals with how content overflow is handled within a box and creates a scroll bar if it is needed?
a. overflow=scroll
b. overflow=visible
c. overflow=none
d. overflow=auto

4. What does the position: absolute attribute accomplish?
a. The div becomes part of the page flow and moves with the content surrounding it.
b. The div adjusts its position relative to the browser.
c. The div stays in the absolute left corner of the browser.
d. The div stays in the right hand corner of the browser.

9.2 Float and Clear

In this section we are going to discuss further use of CSS and HTML to lay out webpages or web documents.

In presenting the topic, the idea is to partition the whole document page into logical divisions or divs. Each partition is treated as a logical division, having its own <div id= "name".

Please use the code below as a reference:

```
<?xml version="1.0" encoding="UTF-8"?>
<!DOCTYPE html PUBLIC "-//W3C//DTD XHTML 1.0 Strict//EN"
"http://www.w3.org/TR/xhtml1/DTD/xhtml1-strict.dtd">
<html xmlns="http://www.w3.org/1999/xhtml" xml:lang="en" lang="en">
<head>
    <title>Inline div vs. Block div</title>
    <style type="text/css">
        #div1, #div2
            {
                font-family: arial;
                font-size: .8em;
                width: 400px;

            }
        #footer p
            {
                font-size: .65em;
                font-family: georgia;
                text-align: center;

            }
        #header h1
            {
                font-family: arial;
                font-size: 1.4em;
                font-weight: bold;
                text-align: center;

            }
    </style>
</head>
<body>
    <div id="header">
        <h1>This is a Simple, Example Layout</h1>
    </div>
    <div id="div1">
            Cras euismod nunc non turpis accumsan eu dictum nibh
adipiscing. Etiam et hendrerit massa. Morbi pretium, magna sed
consectetur hendrerit, dolor dolor sagittis nibh, id ullamcorper
leo dui sit amet diam. Sed in urna sapien, eget tempus elit. Fusce
sed mattis urna. Quisque ac ipsum sapien, quis aliquet erat.
            Cras euismod nunc non turpis accumsan eu dictum nibh
adipiscing. Etiam et hendrerit massa. Morbi pretium, magna sed
consectetur hendrerit, dolor dolor sagittis nibh, id ullamcorper
leo dui sit amet diam. Sed in urna sapien, eget tempus elit. Fusce
sed mattis urna. Quisque ac ipsum sapien, quis aliquet erat.
            Cras euismod nunc non turpis accumsan eu dictum nibh
adipiscing. Etiam et hendrerit massa. Morbi pretium, magna sed
```

```
consectetur hendrerit, dolor dolor sagittis nibh, id ullamcorper
leo dui sit amet diam. Sed in urna sapien, eget tempus elit. Fusce
sed mattis urna. Quisque ac ipsum sapien, quis aliquet erat.
        Cras euismod nunc non turpis accumsan eu dictum nibh
adipiscing. Etiam et hendrerit massa. Morbi pretium, magna sed
consectetur hendrerit, dolor dolor sagittis nibh, id ullamcorper
leo dui sit amet diam. Sed in urna sapien, eget tempus elit. Fusce
sed mattis urna. Quisque ac ipsum sapien, quis aliquet erat.
    </div>
    <div id="footer">
    <p>Copyright 2011 | Mark Lassoff | LearnToProgram.tv
    </p>
    </div>
</body>
</html>
```

The first logical division we will alter is our header div. In the header div we have an h1
tag that functions as the title. In the CSS portion, we have changed the font to arial, set
the font size to 140% of the average font size, set to bold and aligned to the center.

To introduce the styling, we'll refer to the element inside the div and specify
modifications using a descendant selector. For our activity, we will set the h1 of the
header div. The selector would be:

```
#header h1
```

This instructs the browser to style the header according to the attributes found within
the descendant selector under #header h1.

Let us now define the CSS attributes. First is the footer p descendant selector. Set the
font size of the footer to 65% of the default style font, the font type to Georgia and text
alignment to center. This will set the footer apart from the other text.

Div1 and div2 boxes are displayed one on top of the other vertically. If you want to
place them next to one another, you need to create a container div that encompasses
the entire page. This will contain all the elements of the page so they don't move
separately within the page. If you set the width of the container to 800px, it means that
everything in the container can only be a width of up to 800 pixels. This will help you
keep the header and footer in place when the user expands the browser page.

You can now also set the background color of the entire page in the container div. We
will set it to #dddddd for a nice grey color.

Now that all of the content is in the container div, you need to make sure there are no
margins in the body. Set the margin rule in body to 0 pixels. This ensures that the entire
page is now within the container div.

Sometimes, however, other elements can still cause issues with the style. In our case,
the h1 element is causing a margin on the top of our document. In order to remove this,
set the margin-top to 0. That closes the margin gap on the top.

You can also center the container div on the page by setting our margin rule to:

```
margin: 0 auto;
```

This centers the div on the page. As you change the page width, the div will remain centered. You can also change the height of the container box using the height rule.

If you want to place the content boxes next to one another, you have to take each div and use the float rule to make them float side by side. Let us set div1 and div2 to float as follows:

```
float: right;
```

and:

```
float: left;
```

If you have set the margins of these divs separately, they may not fit into the margin of the container when they are placed side by side. You need to adjust the margins to accommodate the containers. In this example, we will set each div to 395 pixels so they fit within the 800 pixels of the container.

Unfortunately, this now has caused a problem with the footer div. After we set div1 and div2 to the left and to the right, the footer div no longer appeared at the bottom. You can use the clear attribute to fix this.

```
clear: both;
```

This will make sure the footer clears both divs and ends up at the bottom of our page. The float and clear rules helped create a more professional layout of the HTML page.

This is what our code looks like using the float and clear attributes:

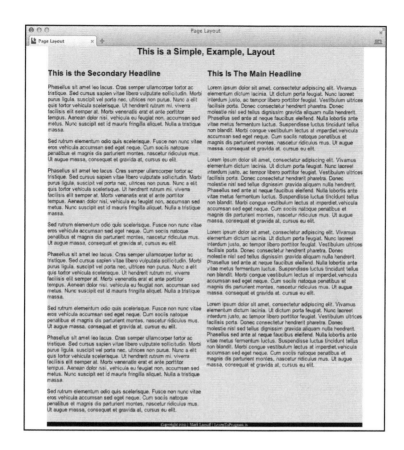

Code Listing: Float and Clear

```
<?xml version="1.0" encoding="UTF-8"?>
<!DOCTYPE html PUBLIC "-//W3C//DTD XHTML 1.0 Strict//EN"
"http://www.w3.org/TR/xhtml1/DTD/xhtml1-strict.dtd">
<html xmlns="http://www.w3.org/1999/xhtml" xml:lang="en" lang="en">
<head>
    <title>Page Layout</title>
    <style type="text/css">
        body
            {
                margin: 0px;
            }
        #container
            {
                width: 800px;
                background-color: #dddddd;
                margin: 0 auto;


            }
        #div1, #div2
            {
                font-family: arial;
```

```
                    font-size: .8em;
            }
        #div2
            {
                    float: left;
                    width: 395px;
            }
        #div1
            {
                    width: 395px;
                    float: right;
            }
        #footer
            {
                    background-color: black;
                    color: white;
                    clear: both;
            }
        #footer p
            {
                    font-size: .65em;
                    font-family: georgia;
                    text-align: center;


            }
        #header h1
            {
                    font-family: arial;
                    font-size: 1.4em;
                    font-weight: bold;
                    text-align: center;
                    margin-top: 0px;
            }
    </style>
</head>
<body>
    <div id="container">
    <div id="header">
        <h1>This is a Simple, Example, Layout</h1>
    </div>
    <div id="div1">
        <h2>This Is The Main Headline</h2>
        <p>Lorem ipsum dolor sit amet, consectetur adipiscing elit.
Vivamus elementum dictum lacinia. Ut dictum porta feugiat. Nunc
laoreet interdum justo, ac tempor libero porttitor feugiat.
Vestibulum ultrices facilisis porta. Donec consectetur hendrerit
pharetra. Donec molestie nisl sed tellus dignissim gravida aliquam
nulla hendrerit. Phasellus sed ante at neque faucibus eleifend.
Nulla lobortis ante vitae metus fermentum luctus. Suspendisse
luctus tincidunt tellus non blandit. Morbi congue vestibulum lectus
at imperdiet.vehicula accumsan sed eget neque. Cum sociis natoque
penatibus et magnis dis parturient montes, nascetur ridiculus mus.
Ut augue massa, consequat et gravida at, cursus eu elit.</p>
        <p> Lorem ipsum dolor sit amet, consectetur adipiscing
elit. Vivamus elementum dictum lacinia. Ut dictum porta feugiat.
Nunc laoreet interdum justo, ac tempor libero porttitor feugiat.
Vestibulum ultrices facilisis porta. Donec consectetur hendrerit
pharetra. Donec molestie nisl sed tellus dignissim gravida aliquam
nulla hendrerit. Phasellus sed ante at neque faucibus eleifend.
Nulla lobortis ante vitae metus fermentum luctus. Suspendisse
```

208

luctus tincidunt tellus non blandit. Morbi congue vestibulum lectus at imperdiet.vehicula accumsan sed eget neque. Cum sociis natoque penatibus et magnis dis parturient montes, nascetur ridiculus mus. Ut augue massa, consequat et gravida at, cursus eu elit.</p>
    <p>Lorem ipsum dolor sit amet, consectetur adipiscing elit. Vivamus elementum dictum lacinia. Ut dictum porta feugiat. Nunc laoreet interdum justo, ac tempor libero porttitor feugiat. Vestibulum ultrices facilisis porta. Donec consectetur hendrerit pharetra. Donec molestie nisl sed tellus dignissim gravida aliquam nulla hendrerit. Phasellus sed ante at neque faucibus eleifend. Nulla lobortis ante vitae metus fermentum luctus. Suspendisse luctus tincidunt tellus non blandit. Morbi congue vestibulum lectus at imperdiet.vehicula accumsan sed eget neque. Cum sociis natoque penatibus et magnis dis parturient montes, nascetur ridiculus mus. Ut augue massa, consequat et gravida at, cursus eu elit.</p>
    <p> Lorem ipsum dolor sit amet, consectetur adipiscing elit. Vivamus elementum dictum lacinia. Ut dictum porta feugiat. Nunc laoreet interdum justo, ac tempor libero porttitor feugiat. Vestibulum ultrices facilisis porta. Donec consectetur hendrerit pharetra. Donec molestie nisl sed tellus dignissim gravida aliquam nulla hendrerit. Phasellus sed ante at neque faucibus eleifend. Nulla lobortis ante vitae metus fermentum luctus. Suspendisse luctus tincidunt tellus non blandit. Morbi congue vestibulum lectus at imperdiet.vehicula accumsan sed eget neque. Cum sociis natoque penatibus et magnis dis parturient montes, nascetur ridiculus mus. Ut augue massa, consequat et gravida at, cursus eu elit.</p>
    </div>
    <div id="div2">
        <h2>This is the Secondary Headline</h2>
        Phasellus sit amet leo lacus. Cras semper ullamcorper tortor ac tristique. <span>Sed cursus sapien vitae libero vulputate sollicitudin. Morbi purus ligula, suscipit vel porta nec, ultrices non purus.</span> Nunc a elit quis tortor vehicula scelerisque. Ut hendrerit rutrum mi, viverra facilisis elit semper at. Morbi venenatis erat et ante porttitor tempus. Aenean dolor nisi, vehicula eu feugiat non, accumsan sed metus. Nunc suscipit est id mauris fringilla aliquet. Nulla a tristique massa. <p>Sed rutrum elementum odio quis scelerisque. Fusce non nunc vitae eros vehicula accumsan sed eget neque. Cum sociis natoque penatibus et magnis dis parturient montes, nascetur ridiculus mus. Ut augue massa, consequat et gravida at, cursus eu elit.</p>
        Phasellus sit amet leo lacus. Cras semper ullamcorper tortor ac tristique. <span>Sed cursus sapien vitae libero vulputate sollicitudin. Morbi purus ligula, suscipit vel porta nec, ultrices non purus.</span> Nunc a elit quis tortor vehicula scelerisque. Ut hendrerit rutrum mi, viverra facilisis elit semper at. Morbi venenatis erat et ante porttitor tempus. Aenean dolor nisi, vehicula eu feugiat non, accumsan sed metus. Nunc suscipit est id mauris fringilla aliquet. Nulla a tristique massa. <p>Sed rutrum elementum odio quis scelerisque. Fusce non nunc vitae eros vehicula accumsan sed eget neque. Cum sociis natoque penatibus et magnis dis parturient montes, nascetur ridiculus mus. Ut augue massa, consequat et gravida at, cursus eu elit.</p>
        Phasellus sit amet leo lacus. Cras semper ullamcorper tortor ac tristique. <span>Sed cursus sapien vitae libero vulputate sollicitudin. Morbi purus ligula, suscipit vel porta nec, ultrices non purus.</span> Nunc a elit quis tortor vehicula scelerisque. Ut hendrerit rutrum mi, viverra facilisis elit semper at. Morbi venenatis erat et ante porttitor tempus. Aenean dolor nisi, vehicula eu feugiat non, accumsan sed metus. Nunc suscipit est id

mauris fringilla aliquet. Nulla a tristique massa. <p>Sed rutrum
elementum odio quis scelerisque. Fusce non nunc vitae eros vehicula
accumsan sed eget neque. Cum sociis natoque penatibus et magnis dis
parturient montes, nascetur ridiculus mus. Ut augue massa,
consequat et gravida at, cursus eu elit.</p>

    Phasellus sit amet leo lacus. Cras semper ullamcorper
tortor ac tristique. Sed cursus sapien vitae libero vulputate
sollicitudin. Morbi purus ligula, suscipit vel porta nec, ultrices
non purus. Nunc a elit quis tortor vehicula scelerisque. Ut
hendrerit rutrum mi, viverra facilisis elit semper at. Morbi
venenatis erat et ante porttitor tempus. Aenean dolor nisi,
vehicula eu feugiat non, accumsan sed metus. Nunc suscipit est id
mauris fringilla aliquet. Nulla a tristique massa. <p>Sed rutrum
elementum odio quis scelerisque. Fusce non nunc vitae eros vehicula
accumsan sed eget neque. Cum sociis natoque penatibus et magnis dis
parturient montes, nascetur ridiculus mus. Ut augue massa,
consequat et gravida at, cursus eu elit.</p>

```
        </div> <!-- End Div2 -->
        <div id="footer">
        <p>Copyright 2011 | Mark Lassoff | LearnToProgram.tv</p>
        </div> <!-- End footer -->
        </div> <!-- End Container -->
</body>
</html>
```

In this example, CSS has helped us create a professional layout for our page. Observe
how the header and footer divs were set apart through div1 and div2.

Questions for Review

1. How does a container div alter a layout?
a. It sets the attributes for divs that haven't been set already.
b. It contains all the layout in a single box.
c. It places the layout in an inline element.
d. It doesn't do anything.

2. What attribute do you use to center the div on the page?
a. margin: auto;
b. margin: 0;
c. margin: center;
d. margin: 0 auto;

3.. What attribute would you use to line divs up next to one another?
a. margin
b. width
c. float
d. clear

9.3 Creating a CSS Navigation Bar

One of the most complicated aspects of HTML is creating a navigation bar. In this section we will be using CSS to create a navigation bar. Many HTML developers are taught how to create navigation bars using individual graphics with rollover effects, however, that is not the best or most efficient way.

This method of creating a navigation bar is executed by using a combination of HTML and CSS. In the HTML document, we have created an unordered list and placed links to our favorite sites within the list.

```
<html>
<head>
<title>
</title>
</head>
<body>
        <ul>
                <li><a href="url"LearnToProgram</a></li>
                <li><a href="url">Udemy</a></li>
                <li><a href="url">UCONN</a></li>
                <li><a href="url">CNN</a></li>
                <li><a href="url">CNET</a></li>
                <li><a href="url">TWiT</a></li>
        </ul>
```

This is how the list will look when viewed in the browser:

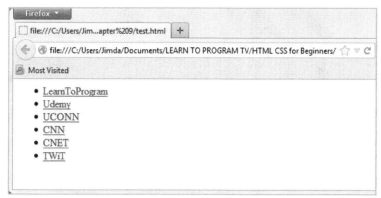

This is an unordered list of example websites. You may use any site you want to for this application exercise. Using CSS, let us turn the unordered list into an actual navigation bar.

First, we place the CSS declaration in the head. Next, remove the bullets and then the underlines, including the color change for visited and unvisited links.

The CSS code to remove the bullets is:

```
ul
```

```
          {
          list-style-type: none;
          }
```

This is now how the unordered list will look:

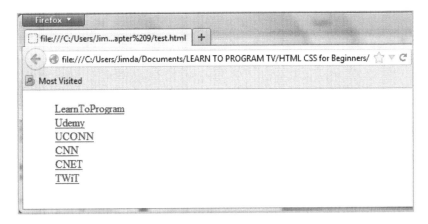

Next we want to eliminate the underline of the links and set the color of the links to black. To do that, change the text-decoration attribute to none. Following is the code to implement the CSS style changes:

```
li a:link, li a:visited
{
               text-decoration: none;
               color: #666666;
}
```

This is how the list would look:

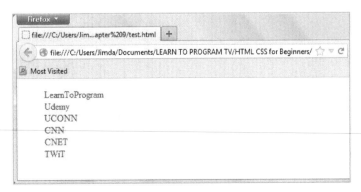

Now decide if you want your navigation bar to be vertical or horizontal. Either way can be achieved by changing the display element.

Setting the display attribute within the li element into block will make a vertical navigation bar. Changing the display's attribute to inline will create a horizontal navigation bar. The following CSS li style attribute:

```
li      {
        display: block;
        }
```

will create a vertical navigation bar as follows:

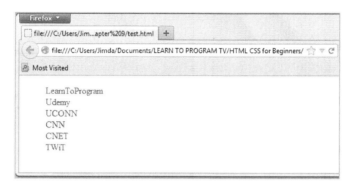

Changing the attribute into **inline** will turn it into a horizontal navigation bar:

```
li      {
        display: inline;
        }
```

Setting the padding for the list items and width at certain values will ensure a pleasant-looking navigation bar. Make sure when you set the navigation bar to horizontal, that you also set the padding of each side and create a negative margin so no white space appears between each list item. For a vertical navigation bar, put in the values shown below:

```
li      {
                display: block;
                padding-top: 15px;
                padding-bottom: 15px;
                width: 170px;
                margin: -2px;
        }
```

This will now change the distances between each list item vertically:

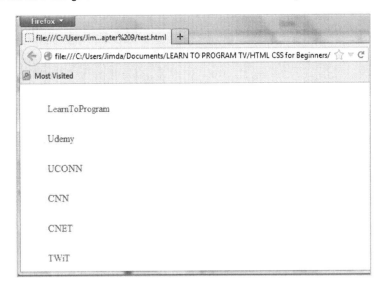

Now you can set the background color of the list items to differentiate the navigation bar from the rest of the page. In our example we set our list background to yellow. To do the same, follow the codes below:

```
li      {
                display: inline;
                padding-top: 15px;
                padding-bottom: 15px;
                width: 150px;
                margin: -2px;
                background-color: yellow;
        }
```

The list item will now look like this when viewed on the browser:

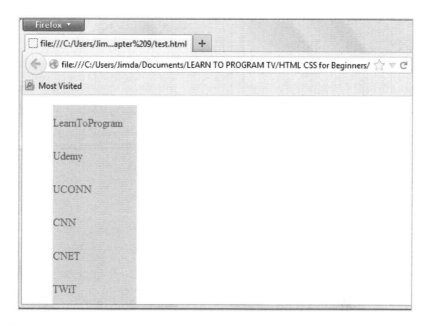

There are a couple of small changes we are going to make to our design. Let's change the font to Georgia, the color to light brown, the font-weight to bold and the font-size to 120% of the default font size.

```
li a:link, li a:visited
{
          text-decoration: none;
          color: #666666;
          font-family: Georgia, times;
          font-weight: bold;
          font-size: 1.2em;
}
```

This is how the list items will look when viewed in the browser:

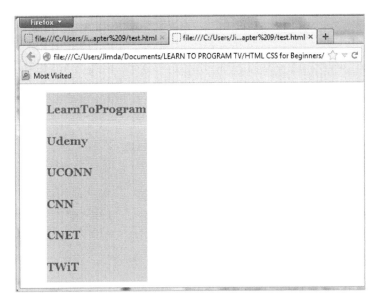

If you want to create a small rollover effect so that the user knows when the cursor is on the specific link, you will once again work with a pseudo-element. This pseudo-element is:

```
li:hover
    {
            background-color: orange;
    }
```

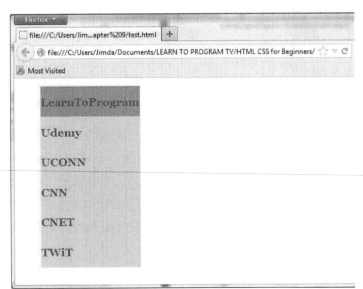

This indicates when the cursor is hovering over the specific list item.

This effect is achieved by changing the background color by means of the pseudo-element. In the above example, when the user hovers the cursor over any link list item, the background color changes to orange.

Following is the code listing for creating a navigation bar. Notice how the padding is set and the width is accommodating all list items.

Code Listing: CSS Navigation Bar

```
<?xml version="1.0" encoding="UTF-8"?>
<!DOCTYPE html PUBLIC "-//W3C//DTD XHTML 1.0 Strict//EN"
"http://www.w3.org/TR/xhtml1/DTD/xhtml1-strict.dtd">
<html xmlns="http://www.w3.org/1999/xhtml" xml:lang="en" lang="en">
<head>
    <title>Inline vs. Block</title>
    <style type="text/css">
        ul
            {
            list-style-type: none;
            margin: 0px;
            padding: 0px;
            }
        li a:link, li a:visited
            {
            text-decoration: none;
            color: #666666;
            font: georgia, times;
            font-weight: bold;
            font-size: 1.2em;
            }
        li
            {
            display: inline;
            padding-top: 8px;
            padding-bottom: 8px;
            padding-left: 15px;
            padding-right: 15px;
            background-color: yellow;
            width: 150px;
            margin: -2px;
            }
        li:hover
            {
            background-color: orange;
            }
    </style>
</head>
<body>
    <ul>
        <li><a
href="http://www.learntoprogram.tv">LearnToProgram</a></li>
        <li><a href="http://www.udemy.com">Udemy</a></li>
        <li><a href="http://www.uconn.edu">UCONN</a></li>
        <li><a href="http://www.cnn.com">CNN</a></li>
        <li><a href="http://www.cnet.com">CNET</a></li>
        <li><a href="http://www.twit.tv">TWiT</a></li>
    </ul>
</body>
```

```html
</html>
```

This is how the horizontal navigation bar will end up looking. With a few tweaks, you create an entirely different looking, but similarly functional, navigation bar. Observe how links display a orange background when hovered over.

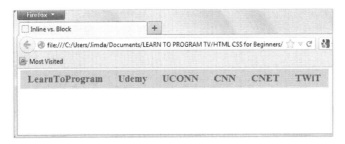

Questions for Review

1. How do you start your navigation bar in HTML?
a. By creating a table of links.
b. By creating a paragraph that contains links.
c. By creating an unordered list full of links.
d. By starting with a header.

2. What attribute would you use to take the bullets out of the list?
a. list-style-type: none
b. list-style-type: no bullets
c. list: none
d. list-style-bullet: no

Chapter 9 Summary

In this chapter we discussed inline vs. block elements and how they are used. You also learned how to use the float and clear attributes in order to properly lay out the content in the CSS box model.

We also discussed how to create a CSS navigation bar. CSS allows you to create a flexible, functional and good-looking navigation bar compared to those created using HTML.

Chapter 9 Lab Exercises

1) Create a correct and standard-compliant XHTML basic document structure. Inside the <title> element place the text Lab 9: Forms.

2) Open the lab_start.html file provided with the course. Notice that there is no CSS in the file and only the HTML is present.

3) Add id attributes to the divs so that you may identify them in the CSS code that you are about to write.

4) Using the techniques and skills demonstrated, reproduce the layout pictured below. Make sure the entire site is 960 px wide and centered within the web browser. You may have to add a container <div> and set the margins for the body selector to 0.

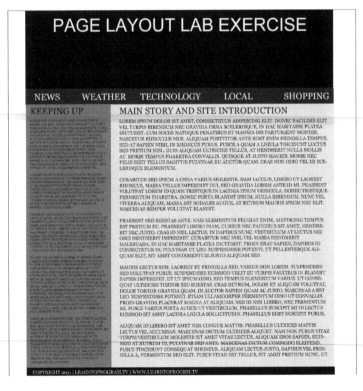

5) Using the techniques demonstrated in the chapter, make the navigation bar interactive by changing the background color of each <li> when the user hovers over it.

Lab Solution

```
<!DOCTYPE HTML PUBLIC "-//W3C//DTD HTML 4.01//EN"
    "http://www.w3.org/TR/html4/strict.dtd"
```

```
    >
<html lang="en">
<head>
    <title>Lab 9: Page Layout</title>
</head>
<style>
        #container
            {
                width: 960px;
                margin: 0px auto;
                height: 400px;
            }
        #div1
            {
                font-family: arial;
                font-size: 1em;
                color: white;
                height: 80px;
                border: none;
                background-color: #000000;
                text-align: center;
                margin-top: -21px;
                padding-bottom: 75px;
            }
        #div2
            {
                font-family: times new roman;
                font-size: 1.2em;
                padding-left: 50px;
                padding-right: 50px;
                padding-top: 25px;
                padding-bottom: 10px;
                color: white;
                height: 25px;
                border: none;
                background-color: #0000FF;
            }
        #div3
            {
                background-color: #aaaaaa;
                width: 280px;
                font-size: 0.6em;
                padding-left: 10px;
                padding-right: 10px;
                text-wrap: normal;
                height: auto;
                float: left;
            }
        #div4
            {
                background-color: #dddddd;
                width: 620px;
                font-size: 0.9em;
                padding-left: 20px;
                padding-right: 20px;
                text-wrap: normal;
                height: 1122px;
                float: right;
                padding-bottom: 10px;
            }
```

```css
        #div5
            {
                clear: both;
                background-color: black;
                color: white;
                padding-left: 20px;
            }
        #div5 a:link
            {
                color: white;
                text-decoration: none;

            }
        ul
                {
                list-style-type: none;
                margin: 0px;
                padding: 0px;
            }
        li a:link, li a:visited
                {
                text-decoration: none;
                color: #FFFFFF;
                font: georgia, times;
                font-weight: bold;
                font-size: .75em;
                 width: 960px;
                    }
        li
                {
                display: inline;
                padding-top: 10px;
                padding-bottom: 8px;
                padding-left: 50.05px;
                padding-right: 50.05px;
                width: 960px;
                margin: -2px auto;
                    }
        li:hover
                {
                text-decoration: underline;
                    }
        html
            {
                text-transform: uppercase;
            }
</style>
<body>
    <div id="container">
    <div id="div1">
        <h1>PAGE LAYOUT LAB EXERCISE</h1>
    </div>
    <div id="div2">
        <ul>
            <li><a href="#">NEWS</a></li>
            <li><a href="#">WEATHER</a></li>
            <li><a href="#">TECHNOLOGY</a></li>
            <li><a href="#">LOCAL</a></li>
            <li><a href="#">SHOPPING</a></li>
        </ul>
```

```
    </div>
    <div id="div3">
        <h2>KEEPING UP</h2>
        <p>Lorem ipsum dolor sit amet, consectetur adipiscing elit.
In quis sapien metus. Etiam libero arcu, ornare venenatis lobortis
sed, faucibus sit amet quam. Proin augue ante, blandit nec blandit
aliquet, egestas mattis urna. Sed libero erat, pellentesque vel
lacinia sed, semper eu massa. Mauris id ante nisi, ut ornare velit.
Nulla quis diam quis dolor tempor molestie a sit amet ligula. Ut
vitae mollis eros. Cras blandit eros sit amet ligula lacinia id
semper dui imperdiet. Etiam vel orci non sem fringilla euismod at
sit amet sem. Nullam scelerisque nisl nec lorem mollis dignissim.
Sed varius lectus et augue elementum sed venenatis dui scelerisque.
Proin iaculis odio a est facilisis id pellentesque odio semper.
Donec feugiat sodales dolor, id pharetra tellus dapibus id.</p>

<p>Suspendisse nisl eros, consectetur vel tempus ut, mattis eget
dui. Nunc malesuada lacus orci, et volutpat leo. Maecenas
imperdiet, ipsum in interdum mollis, magna tellus mattis odio, a
viverra lacus dolor ut mi. Suspendisse porttitor facilisis augue,
id laoreet ligula vehicula sed. Proin nec nunc lacus. Phasellus
posuere nulla id tortor venenatis iaculis. Phasellus fermentum
mattis mattis. Pellentesque vulputate, lorem ut suscipit vulputate,
nisl eros lacinia nibh, et congue diam est eu ipsum. Proin aliquet
pulvinar semper. Nam lobortis posuere nibh non vulputate. Sed
fringilla, odio quis suscipit facilisis, magna erat egestas massa,
id rutrum enim mi id massa. Integer non urna nisl. Pellentesque
habitant morbi tristique senectus et netus et malesuada fames ac
turpis egestas. In id tellus elit. Suspendisse potenti. Suspendisse
rhoncus diam quis nisl vestibulum a tincidunt diam fermentum.</p>

<p>Sed erat purus, scelerisque sed mollis vitae, congue id nisl.
Fusce tempor arcu at lorem gravida aliquam. Class aptent taciti
sociosqu ad litora torquent per conubia nostra, per inceptos
himenaeos. Fusce eleifend ipsum at eros accumsan eu fringilla odio
fermentum. Nunc fringilla porta purus, vitae iaculis velit
hendrerit sit amet. Integer vitae dapibus orci. Pellentesque vitae
purus eu justo accumsan eleifend. Pellentesque vitae purus ante.
Aliquam erat volutpat. Nam fermentum, mauris vel tincidunt
volutpat, purus purus malesuada libero, eget porttitor massa metus
nec libero. Suspendisse potenti. Phasellus at velit nec sapien
consequat consectetur. Ut bibendum ornare hendrerit. Aenean sit
amet lorem nec purus rhoncus blandit commodo at neque. Proin
sollicitudin sodales sodales. Pellentesque pharetra bibendum
semper.</p>

<p>Sed eget dignissim sem. Curabitur consequat nisl eu sem eleifend
tristique. Vestibulum metus augue, vulputate sed consequat vel,
tristique et arcu. Nam suscipit libero non augue laoreet eu
malesuada massa bibendum. Donec sed mi libero. Nunc id purus quam,
eu convallis arcu. Nunc non neque sed enim ornare mollis et id
magna. Pellentesque est nibh, dapibus sollicitudin dignissim sit
amet, vehicula accumsan neque. Sed posuere tempus mi a ultrices.
Maecenas id magna dui. Sed ut nunc neque, sit amet tincidunt mi.
Etiam lobortis lacus venenatis enim consequat id ornare erat
aliquam. Donec lacus nisi, pretium non sodales ac, accumsan sed
magna. Duis adipiscing nulla non sapien volutpat sed posuere purus
consectetur.</p>
```

```
<p>Vivamus mattis augue quis magna congue convallis. Vestibulum
sollicitudin lectus a urna faucibus et elementum lacus egestas.
Proin quis ipsum sit amet purus eleifend mattis. Integer id lectus
vitae urna elementum tempus. Nunc bibendum facilisis magna, sed
ultrices urna rutrum eu. Aenean vitae nibh dolor, a tempor tortor.
Maecenas eleifend, augue eleifend rhoncus accumsan, odio diam
elementum erat, nec egestas mi nisl quis massa. Mauris eu ultrices
nisl. Cras fringilla lectus ac dui volutpat egestas.</p>
    </div>
    <div id="div4">
        <h2>MAIN STORY AND SITE INTRODUCTION</h2>
        <p>Lorem ipsum dolor sit amet, consectetur adipiscing elit.
In quis sapien metus. Etiam libero arcu, ornare venenatis lobortis
sed, faucibus sit amet quam. Proin augue ante, blandit nec blandit
aliquet, egestas mattis urna. Sed libero erat, pellentesque vel
lacinia sed, semper eu massa. Mauris id ante nisi, ut ornare velit.
Nulla quis diam quis dolor tempor molestie a sit amet ligula. Ut
vitae mollis eros. Cras blandit eros sit amet ligula lacinia id
semper dui imperdiet. Etiam vel orci non sem fringilla euismod at
sit amet sem. Nullam scelerisque nisl nec lorem mollis dignissim.
Sed varius lectus et augue elementum sed venenatis dui scelerisque.
Proin iaculis odio a est facilisis id pellentesque odio semper.
Donec feugiat sodales dolor, id pharetra tellus dapibus id.</p>

<p>Suspendisse nisl eros, consectetur vel tempus ut, mattis eget
dui. Nunc malesuada lacus orci, et volutpat leo. Maecenas
imperdiet, ipsum in interdum mollis, magna tellus mattis odio, a
viverra lacus dolor ut mi. Suspendisse porttitor facilisis augue,
id laoreet ligula vehicula sed. Proin nec nunc lacus. Phasellus
posuere nulla id tortor venenatis iaculis. Phasellus fermentum
mattis mattis. Pellentesque vulputate, lorem ut suscipit vulputate,
nisl eros lacinia nibh, et congue diam est eu ipsum. Proin aliquet
pulvinar semper. Nam lobortis posuere nibh non vulputate. Sed
fringilla, odio quis suscipit facilisis, magna erat egestas massa,
id rutrum enim mi id massa. Integer non urna nisl. Pellentesque
habitant morbi tristique senectus et netus et malesuada fames ac
turpis egestas. In id tellus elit. Suspendisse potenti. Suspendisse
rhoncus diam quis nisl vestibulum a tincidunt diam fermentum.</p>

<p>Sed erat purus, scelerisque sed mollis vitae, congue id nisl.
Fusce tempor arcu at lorem gravida aliquam. Class aptent taciti
sociosqu ad litora torquent per conubia nostra, per inceptos
himenaeos. Fusce eleifend ipsum at eros accumsan eu fringilla odio
fermentum. Nunc fringilla porta purus, vitae iaculis velit
hendrerit sit amet. Integer vitae dapibus orci. Pellentesque vitae
purus eu justo accumsan eleifend. Pellentesque vitae purus ante.
Aliquam erat volutpat. Nam fermentum, mauris vel tincidunt
volutpat, purus purus malesuada libero, eget porttitor massa metus
nec libero. Suspendisse potenti. Phasellus at velit nec sapien
consequat consectetur. Ut bibendum ornare hendrerit. Aenean sit
amet lorem nec purus rhoncus blandit commodo at neque. Proin
sollicitudin sodales sodales. Pellentesque pharetra bibendum
semper.</p>

<p>Sed eget dignissim sem. Curabitur consequat nisl eu sem eleifend
tristique. Vestibulum metus augue, vulputate sed consequat vel,
tristique et arcu. Nam suscipit libero non augue laoreet eu
malesuada massa bibendum. Donec sed mi libero. Nunc id purus quam,
eu convallis arcu. Nunc non neque sed enim ornare mollis et id
magna. Pellentesque est nibh, dapibus sollicitudin dignissim sit
```

amet, vehicula accumsan neque. Sed posuere tempus mi a ultrices.
Maecenas id magna dui. Sed ut nunc neque, sit amet tincidunt mi.
Etiam lobortis lacus venenatis enim consequat id ornare erat
aliquam. Donec lacus nisi, pretium non sodales ac, accumsan sed
magna. Duis adipiscing nulla non sapien volutpat sed posuere purus
consectetur.</p>

<p>Vivamus mattis augue quis magna congue convallis. Vestibulum
sollicitudin lectus a urna faucibus et elementum lacus egestas.
Proin quis ipsum sit amet purus eleifend mattis. Integer id lectus
vitae urna elementum tempus. Nunc bibendum facilisis magna, sed
ultrices urna rutrum eu. Aenean vitae nibh dolor, a tempor tortor.
Maecenas eleifend, augue eleifend rhoncus accumsan, odio diam
elementum erat, nec egestas mi nisl quis massa. Mauris eu ultrices
nisl. Cras fringilla lectus ac dui volutpat egestas.</p>
    </div>
    <div id="div5">
        <p>COPYRIGHT 2011 | MARK LASSOFF | <a
href="http://www.learntoprogram.tv">WWW.LEARNTOPROGRAM.TV</a></p>
    </div>
    </div>
</body>
</html>

Course Review

Hopefully this course has helped you achieve your objectives for learning HTML and CSS. The primary objective of this course was to help you start off your web development skills so that you can produce your own websites. After reading this course and performing the labs, you should be able to create websites that are both functional and stylish.

If you wish to consider learning web development, there are many different options that you can pursue. Javascript is a terrific web development language and is great for creating dynamic web applications. PHP is another great language to learn because it helps you manage data on your website.

Finally, if you are interested in a website that can change content without any page refresh, you might want to consider AJAX. This technology, which stands for Asynchronous Javascript and XML, will allow you to create a smooth website that functions similarly to a desktop application.

By completing this course you have taken the first step into a much wider world of web development. Whether you choose to continue on or not, the skills you have developed will hopefully help you create the exact website you are looking for.

Appendix A: HTML5 Tag Table

Tag	Explanation
<a> </a>	Anchor or link
<abbr> </abbr>	Abbreviation
<address> </address>	Address or authors of the document
<area >	Client side image map
<article></article>	Article
<aside></aside>	Tangential content
<audio></audio>	Audio stream
<b> </b>	Bold
<base>	Base URL paths for elements in the document
<bdo> </bdo>	Bi-directional algorithm
<blockquote> </blockquote>	Long quotation
<body> </body>	Body of the page
 	Line break
<button> </button>	HTML form button
<canvas></canvas>	Canvas for dynamic graphics
<!-- -->	Comment
<caption> </caption>	Table caption
<cite> </cite>	Citation
<code> </code>	Code reference
<col>	Table column
<colgroup> </colgroup>	Table column grouping
<command>	Command or action on the page
<!doctype>	Document type definition
<datagrid></datagrid>	Data grid
<datalist></datalist>	Predefined options for other controls
<dd> </dd>	Definition list description or span of discourse

Tag	Explanation
<del> </del>	Deleted text
<details></details>	Additional on-demand information
<dfn> </dfn>	Definition
<dialog></dialog>	Conversation
<div> </div>	Logical division
<dl> </dl>	Description list
<dt> </dt>	Definition list term or dialog speaker
<em> </em>	Emphasis
<embed>	Embedded element for plugins
<fieldset> </fieldset>	Form controls group
<figure></figure>	Figure with optional caption
<footer></footer>	Footer of the page
<form> </form>	Form
<h1> </h1>	First level headline
<h2> </h2>	Second level headline
<h3> </h3>	Third level headline
<h4> </h4>	Fourth level headline
<h5> </h5>	Fifth level headline
<h6> </h6>	Sixth level headline
<head> </head>	Head of the document
<header></header>	Header of a page
<hgroup></hgroup>	Heading group
<hr>	Horizontal rule
<html> </html>	Root element of a webpage
<i> </i>	Italics text style
<iframe> </iframe>	Inline frame
<img>	Image
<input>	Input form element

Tag	Explanation
\<input type="button"\>	Button form element
\<input type="checkbox"\>	Checkbox form element
\<input type="color"\>	Color input
\<input type="date"\>	Date input
\<input type="datetime"\>	Global date and time input
\<input type="datetime-local"\>	Local date and time input
\<input type="email"\>	Email address input
\<input type="file"\>	File upload form element
\<input type="hidden"\>	Hidden form field element
\<input type="image"\>	Image form element
\<input type="month"\>	Year and month input
\<input type="number"\>	Number input
\<input type="password"\>	Password form element
\<input type="radio"\>	Radio button form element
\<input type="range"\>	Imprecise number input
\<input type="reset"\>	Reset button form element
\<input type="search"\>	Search field
\<input type="submit"\>	Submit button form element
\<input type="tel"\>	Telephone number input
\<input type="text"\>	Text field form element
\<input type="time"\>	Time input
\<input type="url"\>	URL input
\<input type="week"\>	Year and week input
\<ins\> \</ins\>	Inserted text
\<kbd\> \</kbd\>	Text to be entered by the user
\<keygen\>	Generate secure keys for certificate management
\<label\> \</label\>	Form label
\<legend\> \</legend\>	Form fieldset caption

Tag	Explanation
<li> </li>	List item
<link>	Link to related documents
<map> </map>	Client side image map
<mark></mark>	Marked or highlighted text
<menu> </menu>	List of commands
<meta>	Meta information about the document
<meter></meter>	Scalar gauge
<noscript> </noscript>	Content when scripts aren't available
<object> </object>	Non-standard object
<ol> </ol>	Ordered or numbered list
<optgroup> </optgroup>	Group of options in a select list
<option> </option>	Option in a select list
<output></output>	Result of a form calculation
<p> </p>	Paragraph
<param>	Parameter of an object element
<pre> </pre>	Pre-formatted text
<progress></progress>	Progress indicator
<q> </q>	Short inline quotation
<rp></rp>	Ruby parenthesis
<rt></rt>	Ruby text
<ruby></ruby>	Ruby annotation
<s> </s>	Strikeout text
<samp> </samp>	Sample output
<script> </script>	Scripts
<section></section>	Section of a page
<select> </select>	Select or drop-down menu lists
<small> </small>	Small font size
<source>	Media source

Tag	Explanation
<span> </span>	Generic inline style container
<strong> </strong>	Strong emphasis
<style> </style>	Style sheets
	Subscript
<summary> </summary>	Summary of the DETAILS element contents
	Superscript
<table> </table>	Table
<tbody> </tbody>	Table body rows
<td> </td>	Table cell
<textarea> </textarea>	Multi-line form element
<tfoot> </tfoot>	Table footer rows
<th> </th>	Table header cell
<thead> </thead>	Table header rows
<title> </title>	Title
<tr> </tr>	Table row
<ul> </ul>	Unordered or bulleted list
<var> </var>	Variable or user defined text
<video> </video>	Video or movie embedded in page

2878020R00126

Made in the USA
San Bernardino, CA
13 June 2013